STITCHED CARDS AND GIFT TAGS

for special occasions

STITCHED CARDS AND GIFT TAGS

for special occasions

Carol Phillipson

GUILD OF MASTER CRAFTSMAN PUBLICATIONS

First published 2003 by
Guild of Master Craftsman Publications Ltd,
166 High Street, Lewes,
East Sussex BN7 1XU

Reprinted 2004

ISBN 1 86108 274 6

Publisher: Paul Richardson
Art Director: Ian Smith
Production Manager: Stuart Poole
Managing Editor: Gerrie Purcell
Commissioning Editor: April McCroskie
Editor: Dominique Page
Designer: Chris Halls, Mind's Eye Design, Lewes
Photographer: Anthony Bailey

Typeface: Goudy, Gill Sans and Palatino

Colour origination by Universal Graphics, Pte Ltd, Singapore

Printed and bound by Kyodo Printing Ltd, Singapore

ACKNOWLEDGEMENTS

Once again I must thank Alan, not only for his help and support but also for his enduring patience.

I cannot give enough thanks to Ann for all her enthusiasm and help with stitching and checking the designs.

My thanks go to Fabric Flair for kindly supplying all of the fabrics used for the samples.

My grateful thanks also go to Sally and Coats Crafts UK (+44 (0)1325 394327) for their continuing help in providing almost all of the threads used.

Preparing a book on stitched cards needs blank cards, and I am extremely grateful to Mike Gray and Framecraft Miniatures for supplying those cards with a line around the aperture and Impress Cards for all of the others. Thank you! All of the cards are available by mail order. For details of these cards ring Framecraft Miniatures on +44 (0)1543 360842, and Impress Cards on +44 (0)1986 781422.

CONTENTS

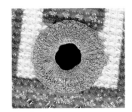

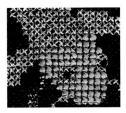

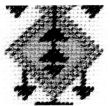

INTRODUCTION

Cards mark an occasion and, for me, a stitched card with the thought and time involved in its creation can help to make it even more special.

When I started to design this collection of stitched cards and gift tags I had two aims. Firstly, and most importantly, I wanted to design cards that would make recipients feel special and could be keepsakes of an occasion; secondly, I wanted the cards to be enjoyable for the stitcher to complete. I hope you will feel I have been successful in achieving these aims.

I have tried to include varied designs that can be adapted for most occasions and, as cards are available in so many shapes, sizes and colours, I hope there is something to please everyone. I particularly like the idea of the bookmark cards, as these can become useful reminders of a special time. Even the gift tags are detailed enough to be stitched individually as small cards.

As most of the designs can be utilized for different occasions, I have chosen not to include messages on the cards, only initials and dates. Instead, I have provided a collection of alphabets that can be used to personalize your stitching with any message or initial. These alphabets have been stitched as samplers, for which the charts are included, to enable you to stitch a whole sampler, if you wish, as a more challenging, larger project. For these three samplers I have detailed the thread amounts required, but I have not done so for the cards and tags, as the amount of each colour used is so slight.

I hope as you look through this book that lots of ideas spring to mind, and you have as much satisfaction in planning and stitching your cards and gift tags as I have had in preparing this book. A lot of pleasure will be gained by anyone receiving one of these cards, of that I am certain, and knowing this will hopefully add to your own enjoyment in its planning and making.

MATERIALS, EQUIPMENT, STITCHES

T he basic tools to enable you to stitch any (or all!) of the designs in this book are simple. I have used fabrics and threads that are readily available, and card blanks can be easily obtained from craft and needlework shops or through mail order. The chapter on Adapting Designs will enable you to change the size of a design to fit an individual card if it is a different size from the one shown in the book. I always back my stitched designs with medium-weight iron-on Vilene before inserting them into the card, as this gives more body to the stitching. Iron-on Vilene is sold by the metre but a full metre backs dozens of cards! You can buy a smaller quantity if you wish.

GENERAL ACCESSORIES

A pair of sharp scissors makes life much easier for the stitcher. I have two pairs of needlework scissors: a small, sharp, pointed pair and a larger pair. The small ones are only to be used for threads and I have even fastened a piece of wool on the handle to remind the rest of the family not to use them for anything else. I use the larger pair for cutting fabric and Vilene. I never use either of these for cutting paper, as this is notorious for blunting even the sharpest scissors.

The use and type of frames is a personal matter. Some stitchers never use one, while others always do. Although it is sometimes tempting not to bother, I always use one because I find the result more pleasing. It certainly minimizes the need for stretching and adjusting.

Although I have a number of different frames, I really only used one for these cards: a small clip-frame. Clip-frames are a collection of lightweight plastic tubes and clips, which can be fitted together to make frames of various sizes. The fabric is simply laid over the frame and tensioners are placed over to keep it in place. A simple twist adjusts the tension. They really have taken the hard work out of putting fabric on a frame and they don't damage or mark the fabric.

A clip-frame

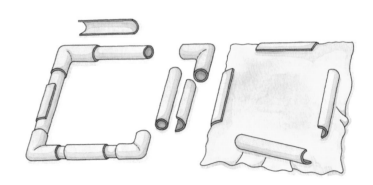

A useful item is a small pair of round magnets which fit on either side of the fabric that is being stitched and trap the chart, so that it stays in view at the edge of the embroidery frame. They also make a safe place to leave a needle. These are certainly invaluable.

A good light is an investment. Although there are many that are specifically designed for embroiderers, I find a good, well-placed spotlight equally acceptable.

Blunt-ended needles should always be used for counted-thread work because they don't split and weaken the threads. I used a size 22 or 24 for all of the cards here. You will also need a beading needle if you intend to fasten beads onto the stitching, and possibly a needle-threader to help to thread this fine needle.

One other essential for making up the cards is a glue stick, obtainable from stationers.

FABRIC

For each item in the book the fabric used is stated, but it can often be substituted. All of the fabrics in the book were supplied by Fabric Flair Limited. I have used mainly 14- and 16-count Aida, 28-count Jobelan (worked over two threads to give a fourteen count) and 22-count Hardanger. If you are using a different fabric, remember that the higher the thread count, the finer the stitching becomes.

THREADS

The majority of the projects in the book are stitched in stranded cotton or Perlé cotton, but I have included some variations, either for the colouring or the texture. I find the wide range of threads and colours available a never-ending source of inspiration.

STITCHES

Although the designs use mainly full or half-cross stitch, I have included some other counted-thread stitches to give a variety of texture and interest. If you have not attempted to use these stitches before, do have the confidence to try them, as they are all easy stitches. However, before stitching the actual card or sampler, it would be wise to try them out on a scrap piece of material so that you can get the stitch and the tension right.

Cross Stitch

First leg of cross-stitch

Completion of cross-stitch

Half-Cross Stitch

Half-cross stitch

Rhodes Stitch

Bring the needle up from the wrong side at 1, go down at 2, come back up at 3, go back down at 4 and repeat this pattern until the stitch is complete. Always work the first stitch in the same direction, starting at the bottom left-hand corner. In the charts, the diagonal line represents the first stitch.

11	13	15	17	19	2
9					4
7					6
5					8
3					10
1	20	18	16	14	12

Eyelet Stitch

Bring the needle up from the wrong side at 1, go down into the centre, come up at 2, go down into the centre, come up at 3 and continue until the stitch is complete. As you work, pull the thread fairly firmly so that the centre hole is clear. Always start at the bottom left-hand corner.

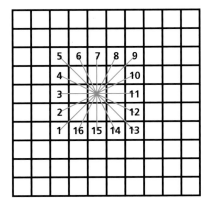

French Knots

Bring the needle through to the right side. Wrap the thread twice round the needle. Pull tightly, then, holding the thread firmly with your free hand, insert the needle through to the back of the work over one thread of the fabric and pull through gently to form the knot which should lie on top of the fabric. To make a bolder, chunkier knot, use a thicker thread.

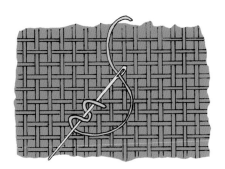

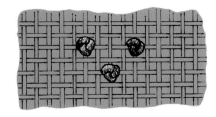

Scottish Stitch

Bring the needle up from the wrong side at 1, go down at 2, come up at 3, go down at 4 and continue until the stitch is complete. Notice that two colours are used here, although if you were using this stitch for another project, it could be stitched using only one colour.

ADAPTING DESIGNS

If you want to change the size of a design to fit another card, this is not difficult to do, but does need to be planned to fit the aperture; nothing could be worse than the design disappearing out of the side of the card because it is too wide or too long!

Charted designs can be worked on any fabric with evenly spaced horizontal and vertical threads. These fabrics are known as evenweave and are said to have a 'count', usually expressed in tpi, i.e. the number of threads the fabric has per inch (2.5cm). So, if you are working over every thread, you will work 14 stitches for every inch. Similarly, if you work on 28-count fabric, but work over two threads (which happens quite often in this book), you are still working 14 stitches in one inch. Stitching a design on a fabric with fewer threads to one inch will enlarge the stitching, but you may then need an extra strand of cotton to cover the canvas or fabric. Always try stitching a small sample and adjust it before starting the main project. Conversely, if the thread count is greater, the work will be smaller, and may need less thread.

I have shown this while stitching individual letters from the medieval sampler. Letter 'B' is stitched on 22-count, letter 'J' on 16-count and letter 'K' on 28-count over two threads, i.e. equivalent to 14-count (see page 154).

To calculate the size of a stitched piece, take the pattern size (stitches) and divide it by the number of threads per inch of the fabric.

As an example, for a design with 22 squares this will be:

2.5cm (1in) when stitched on 22-count (22 divided by 22)
3cm (1¼in) – 18-count (18 divided by 22)
3.8cm (1½in) – 14-count (14 divided by 22)
5.6cm (2⁵⁄₁₆in) – 10-count (10 divided by 22)

Colours are a personal choice. The colours in this book are my choice but they may not be yours, or they just may not suit the recipient of the card. Don't be afraid of changing them. I know from experience that it will usually be more successful if you try to keep the darker tones in my design as the darker tones in yours.

One of my favourite parts of designing is adding the finishing touches and, as you can probably tell, I have thoroughly enjoyed adding accessories to many of these cards. A few beads, a tassel, a twisted cord or a lace-edging costs very little and doesn't take long to add, but it can make a lot of difference to the completed stitching.

I keep containers of beads, ribbons and lace and add to them whenever I come across interesting colours or shapes that I think may become of use in the future. It is sometimes possible to find bargain bags of mixed beads or bundles of narrow ribbon and these often come in useful for finishing small items like cards, which only require small amounts.

MAKING A TASSEL

Take a piece of card slightly longer than the intended length of your tassel. Wrap thread around the card until it is fairly thick (1). Loop a piece of thread between the card and the wound threads at the top, pull it tight and knot it, then cut the threads from the card at the bottom (2). Smooth the threads down and tightly wind a new length of thread to form a tassel (3). Using a needle, thread the end down so that the secured end becomes part of the tassel. Use the thread at the top to fasten the tassel to the stitching (4).

1

2

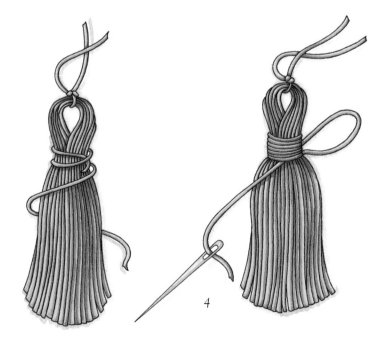

3

4

MAKING A TWISTED CORD

First decide how long your cord needs to be. Always make it a bit longer than you really want it, because it is easy to trim. I cut the threads three times the required length of the cord and half as thick as I would like it to be. Fasten a knot at both ends, then thread one end over a door handle and thread a pencil through the other (1). Keeping the thread fairly taut, twist the pencil round and round the same way until it is tightly twisted. Take hold of the twisted thread in the centre and put the two ends together (2). The cord will automatically twist on itself. Remember to keep it taut as you bring the ends together, then it will twist evenly.

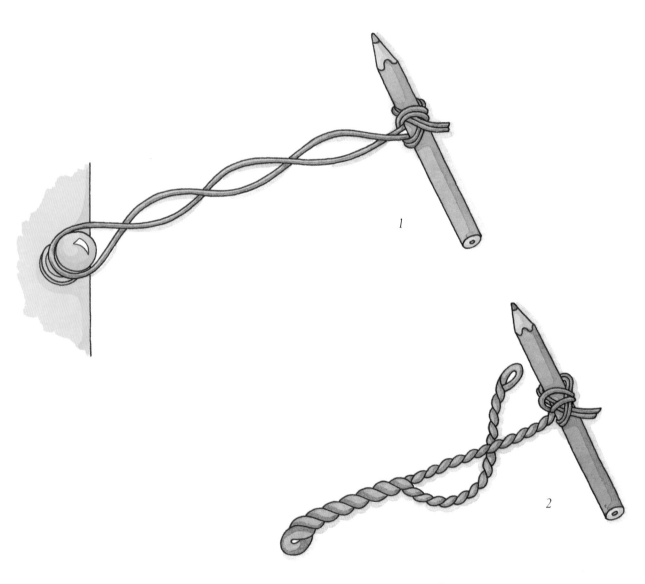

WORKING AND MAKING-UP THE CARD DESIGNS

For each design I have detailed the threads required. Anchor Stranded Cotton colour 342, for instance, is simply listed as Anchor: 342. You will also find examples where I have listed two colours next to each other, such as Anchor: 342/102. This means that one strand of each colour should be used.

Always overcast the edges of the fabric to prevent fraying. If I am going to stitch a few cards with the same count of fabric, I often use a larger piece of material and stitch several designs on the one piece, making sure that each design has enough space around it to allow for making up.

Stitch the design in the centre of the fabric and add any backstitch and beads needed. Check that no loose threads are left on the back, as these may show through. Press the stitching well on the wrong side using a damp cloth.

Cut a piece of iron-on Vilene that is a bit larger than the aperture of the card, then iron it carefully on the back of the stitching using a medium setting.

Using a glue stick, glue the back of the third of the card in which the aperture is cut, then carefully lay it over the stitching so that the design is centred in the card.

Next, either follow the manufacturer's instructions, or glue the third of the card that will cover up the back of the work and stick it in place. I usually place it facedown until the glue is fully dry, with a heavy book on top so that it stays really flat.

THE DESIGNS

Celebrations
page 12

Flowers and Fruits
page 54

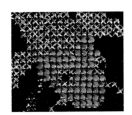

Designs from Japan
page 104

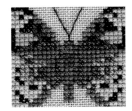

Garden Visitors
page 80

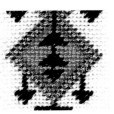

Designs from North America
page 108

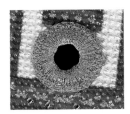

Designs from India
page 92

Gallery of General Card Designs
page 114

Designs from Egypt
page 100

Alphabet Sampler Projects
page 142

CELEBRATIONS

NEW BABY CARDS AND GIFT TAG

This is an occasion when, in my opinion, a personalized, stitched card can add a special welcome to a new baby and give pleasure to the parents. The little rabbit gift tag adds a final thoughtful touch. I attached a pale green ribbon to match the 185 stranded cotton but, as an alternative, the designs could also be stitched in pinks or blues with matching ribbons. The date on the rocking horse could also be changed to a name or, by using a different alphabet from the samplers, could incorporate a name, date and birth weight. The card could be stitched ready for the birth and have the details quickly added before it is sent.

Both of the card designs would also be suitable for celebrating a birthday. The teddy bear could easily be put into a larger card to give space for a name, date or message.

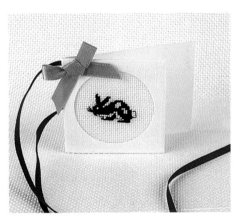

Card details:

Edward Bear	Cream, rectangular aperture 13.9 x 9.5cm (5½ x 3⁷⁄₁₀in)
Rocking horse	Cream, oval aperture 13.9 x 9.5cm (5½ x 3⁷⁄₁₀in)
Rabbit gift tag	White, round aperture 4cm (1½in)

RABBIT GIFT TAG

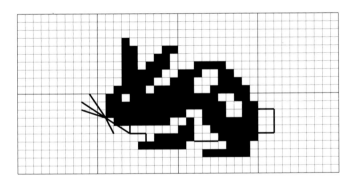

Design size	2.3 x 1.5cm (⁹⁄₁₀ x ⁶⁄₁₀in)
Fabric count	26 holes per inch
Stitch	half-cross
Stitch count	24 x 15
Stitch size	worked over every thread
Number of strands	2

Materials required

⬛	Anchor: 403
⬜	Anchor: 1
⬛	Anchor: 403* **

*Backstitch
**Use 1 strand

EDWARD BEAR CARD

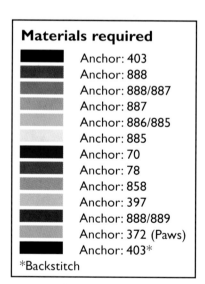

Materials required

■	Anchor: 403
■	Anchor: 888
■	Anchor: 888/887
■	Anchor: 887
■	Anchor: 886/885
■	Anchor: 885
■	Anchor: 70
■	Anchor: 78
■	Anchor: 858
■	Anchor: 397
■	Anchor: 888/889
■	Anchor: 372 (Paws)
■	Anchor: 403*

*Backstitch

Design size	5 x 6.2cm (2 x 2⁹⁄₁₀in)
Fabric count	26 holes per inch
Stitch	half-cross
Stitch count	51 x 63
Stitch size	worked over every thread
Number of strands	2

ROCKING HORSE CARD

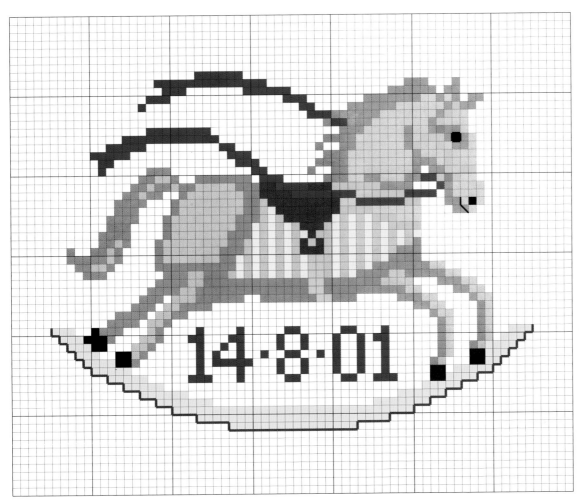

Design size	10.9 x 8.2cm (4³⁄₁₀ x 3³⁄₁₀in)
Fabric	28-count Jobelan
Fabric count	14 holes per inch
Stitch	cross stitch
Stitch count	60 x 45
Stitch size	worked over 2 threads
Number of strands	2 of Stranded Cotton, 1 of Perlé

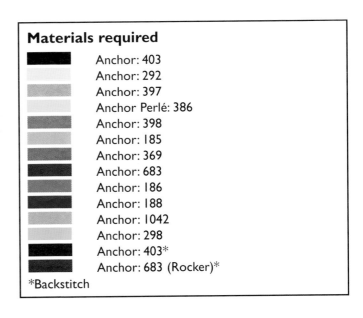

Materials required

	Anchor: 403
	Anchor: 292
	Anchor: 397
	Anchor Perlé: 386
	Anchor: 398
	Anchor: 185
	Anchor: 369
	Anchor: 683
	Anchor: 186
	Anchor: 188
	Anchor: 1042
	Anchor: 298
	Anchor: 403*
	Anchor: 683 (Rocker)*

*Backstitch

CHRISTENING CARD AND GIFT TAG

This special card and gift tag set are perfect to mark such an important family event. Different stitches give texture to the card and the delicate colouring seems appropriate for the occasion. When complete, add a tassel with a twisted cord made using Perlé cotton to match the stitching. The cross is from a pack of charms, which are available from craft and needlework shops or by mail order. A 40cm (16in) length of cream ribbon adds a finishing touch to the gift tag.

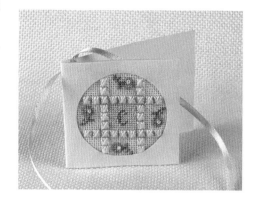

Card details:

Card	Bright white, oval aperture 10.1 x 8.3cm (4 x 3⁵⁄₁₆in)
Gift tag	Bright white, round aperture 4cm (1½in)

Design size	6.1 x 8.5cm (2³⁄₁₀ x 3³⁄₁₀in)
Fabric count	26 holes per inch
Stitch	half-cross
Stitch count	62 x 87
Stitch size	worked over every thread
Number of strands	2

Materials required

	Anchor: 6
	Anchor: 8
	Anchor: 875
	Anchor: 386
	Anchor Perlé: 386
	*
	Mill Hill Petite Glass beads: 00123 x 5

*Denotes start of Rhodes stitch

CHRISTENING CARD

CHRISTENING GIFT TAG

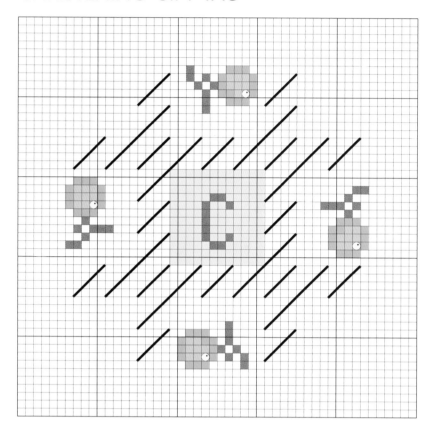

Design size	3.7 x 3.7cm (1½ x 1½in)
Fabric count	26 holes per inch
Stitch	half-cross
Stitch count	38 x 38
Stitch size	worked over every thread
Number of strands	2

Materials required

	Anchor: 6
	Anchor: 8
	Anchor: 875
	Anchor: 386
	*
	Mill Hill Petite Glass beads: 00123 x 4

*Denotes start of Rhodes stitch

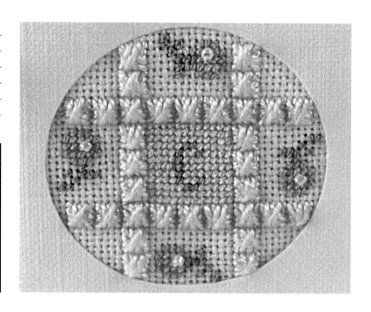

EASTER CARD

This cheerful card, complete with beads and a bow, will brighten up anyone's day, and it will still be there long after the chocolate eggs have disappeared! This design can be worked in any colours, perhaps favourite colours, using up small amounts of leftover threads. I added a yellow bow to give it an extra flourish.

Card details:

White, oval aperture 13.9 x 9.5cm (5½ x 3⁷⁄₁₀in)

Design size	10 x 14cm (3⁷⁄₁₀ x 5½in)
Fabric count	16 holes per inch
Stitch	cross stitch
Stitch count	63 x 88
Stitch size	worked over every thread
Number of strands	2

Materials required

	Anchor: 876
	Anchor: 1036
	Anchor: 879
	Anchor: 1070
	Anchor: 297
	Anchor: 298
	Mill Hill beads: 00525 x 10
	Mill Hill beads: 03035 x 17
	Mill Hill beads: 00123 x 5

EASTER CARD

WEDDING CARD AND GIFT TAGS

Wedding invitations usually arrive some time before the event, giving you chance to stitch a personal card – one which I am sure will be much appreciated and kept for posterity. I used pink, green and silver thread and pearl beads to make this pretty card, then added a ready-made bow and little bells, which, along with the initials and date, make it very distinctive. A length of wedding ribbon glued inside the card at the top and bottom finished it off well. The matching tags would look lovely fastened onto silver wedding giftwrap.

Card details:

Card	White, rectangular aperture 3.9 x 9.5cm (5½ x 3⅞in)
Gift tags	White, circular aperture 4cm (1½in)

WEDDING CARD

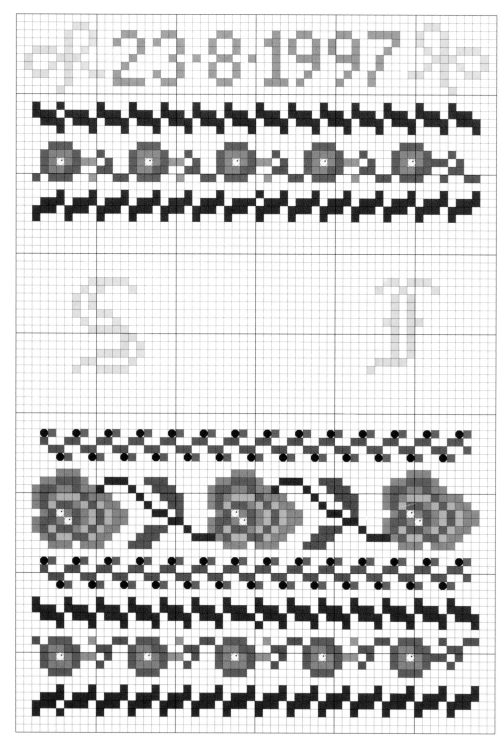

Materials required

	Anchor: Silver Lamé
	Anchor: 214
	Anchor: 215
	Anchor: 217
	Anchor: 970
	Anchor: 969
	Anchor: 968
	Mill Hill beads: 05270 x 27
	Mill Hill beads: 00123 x 10

Design size	9.2 x 13.8cm (3⅗ x 5⅜in)	**Stitch count**	58 x 87
Fabric count	16 holes per inch	**Stitch size**	worked over every thread
Stitch	cross stitch	**Number of strands**	2

GIFT TAG 1

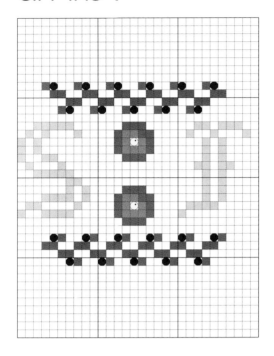

Design size	2.7 x 2.2cm (1⅒ x ⅞in)
Fabric count	26 holes per inch
Stitch	half-cross
Stitch count	28 x 23
Stitch size	worked over every thread
Number of strands	2

GIFT TAG 2

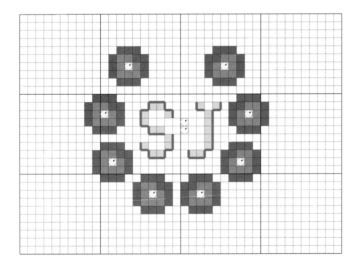

Design size	3.7 x 3.3cm (1⅖ x 1⅒in)
Fabric count	16 holes per inch
Stitch	cross stitch
Stitch count	23 x 21
Stitch size	worked over every thread
Number of strands	2

ROSH HASHANAH CARDS AND GIFT TAG

Rosh Hashanah is celebrated in accordance with the time of the new moon, in late September or early October. It ends with Yom Kippur and represents hope for the following year.

At sunset, after evening prayers and thanks at the Synagogue, candles are lit and blessed bread and wine are eaten and drunk. To illustrate symbolically that the seasons go round in a circle and that it is the start of the New Year, the special loaves, called Challah, are circular in shape. Pieces of apple that have been sweetened with honey are eaten and the customary saying: 'May the New Year bring for us a good and sweet year' is spoken.

Honey is a symbol of good things, so at the time of Rosh Hashanah greetings on cards include bees in addition to apples, candles and the shofar, a musical instrument made from a ram's horn which is used to announce the New Year.

I thought that the two designs used here would be particularly appropriate for Rosh Hashanah celebrations, as well as being suitable for other occasions. I have shown the bee card stitched on 28-count fabric worked over two threads, and as a gift tag worked on 22-count fabric using every thread.

Card details:

Apple card	Red, square aperture 6.7cm (2½in)
Bee card	Rose Lorenzo parchment effect, circular aperture 8.3cm (3¼in)
Gift tag	White, circular aperture 4cm (1½in)

APPLE CARD

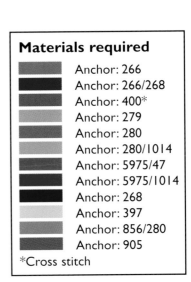

Materials required

	Anchor: 266
	Anchor: 266/268
	Anchor: 400*
	Anchor: 279
	Anchor: 280
	Anchor: 280/1014
	Anchor: 5975/47
	Anchor: 5975/1014
	Anchor: 268
	Anchor: 397
	Anchor: 856/280
	Anchor: 905

*Cross stitch

Design size	5.6 x 5.6cm (2³⁄₁₀ x 2³⁄₁₀in)
Fabric count	28 holes per inch
Stitch	half-cross
Stitch count	57 x 57
Stitch size	worked over every thread
Number of strands	2

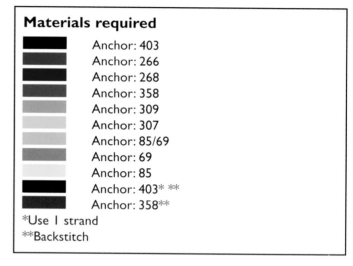

BEE CARD AND GIFT TAG

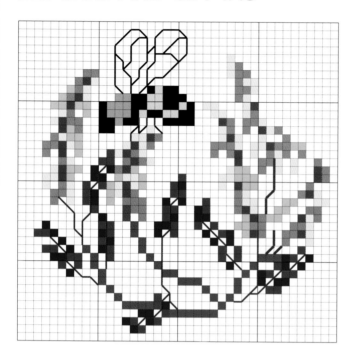

Materials required

■	Anchor: 403
■	Anchor: 266
■	Anchor: 268
■	Anchor: 358
■	Anchor: 309
■	Anchor: 307
■	Anchor: 85/69
■	Anchor: 69
■	Anchor: 85
■	Anchor: 403* **
■	Anchor: 358**

*Use 1 strand
**Backstitch

CARD

Design size	6.7 x 6.9cm (2⁹⁄₁₀ x 2⁷⁄₁₀in)
Fabric	28-count Jobelan
Fabric count	14 holes per inch
Stitch	cross stitch
Stitch count	37 x 38
Stitch size	worked over 2 threads
Number of strands	2

GIFT TAG

Design size	3.6 x 3.7cm (1⁴⁄₁₀ x 1⁵⁄₁₀in)
Fabric count	26 holes per inch
Stitch	half-cross
Stitch count	37 x 38
Stitch size	worked over every thread
Number of strands	2

HANUKKAH CARD

Hanukkah is the Festival of Light, which is held in the Jewish month of Kislev. It starts as soon as three stars can be seen in the sky and lasts for eight days. It symbolizes the Jewish belief in a time when a High Priest only had sufficient oil for the Menorah to burn for one day but a miracle kept it burning for eight days. It is also an

occasion for Jewish people to remember the victory over Antiochus IX, which they believe God helped them to win.

During Hanukkah the candles on a candlestick, called the Menorah, are lit. The Menorah has eight branches and one extra light, known as the Servant, from which the others are lit. The card design here shows the eight-branched Menorah with the servant and the symbolic three stars in the sky. I have added a Star of David, which came from a pack of religious charms. Small gold stars represent the light.

The candlestick is made of a variegated thread, available by mail order from De Haviland threads, but it could be replaced with stranded cotton.

Card details:

White, oval aperture 13.9 x 9.5cm (5½ x 3⁷⁄₁₀in)

Materials required

■	Anchor: 1345 or De Haviland green/blues
▨	Anchor Lamé: 303* or small gold stars
▢	Anchor: 1

*Use 3 strands

Design size	6.4 x 7.6cm (2½ x 3in)
Fabric	28-count Jobelan
Fabric count	14 holes per inch
Stitch	cross stitch
Stitch count	35 x 42
Stitch size	worked over 2 threads
Number of strands	2

DIWALI CARDS

Diwali is the Hindu Festival of Light, which is symbolic of the safe return after fourteen exiled years of King Rama to Ayodhya. It is held in late October or early November, just prior to the new moon, and celebrates the victory of good over evil and hope for the future. Sikhs also celebrate Diwali, but for them the focus is on the release from prison of Guru Hargobind Singh and fifty-two rajas.

Traditionally, before the celebrations begin, people clean their homes and walls are newly whitewashed. Diwali literally means 'a row of lights', so at this time lots of candles and lamps light up the houses, streets and marketplaces. It is also customary for people to purchase new clothes, send their friends sweets and greetings, hold many parties and gatherings, and release fireworks to drive off evil spirits.

I have designed four cards suitable for Diwali. Two of them (those on a blue background) are adapted from Rangoli patterns. These are traditional geometric patterns, sometimes representing lotus flowers, and are usually made on the floor from brightly-coloured sand, flour or chalk. They are drawn at the entrances to homes to welcome both Lakshmi, the goddess of wealth, and visitors to the house.

The third card is devised from Mehndi patterns, which are painstakingly painted on hands and feet using henna leaves mixed with water. These patterns are also used for decorating a bride at a wedding.

For the fourth card I have used a traditional Indian textile block-printing design of leaves and flowers and stitched it on black Jobelan using a variegated thread. The yellow tones in the thread really bring light to the design, so it would be appropriate for Diwali as well as other occasions.

Card details:

Mehndi card	Gold, rectangular aperture 17.1 x 12cm (6⅓₀ x 4⅞₀in)
Rangoli cards	Cream, circular aperture 8.3cm (3¼₀in)
Leaf card	White, rectangular aperture 13.9 x 9.5cm (5½ x 3⅞₀in)

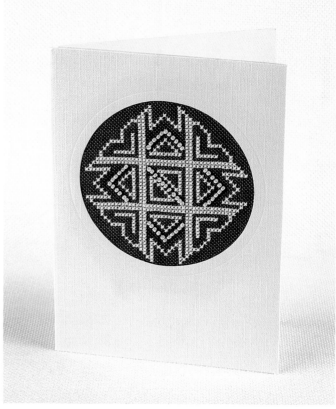

Design size	10.7 x 15.4cm (4²/₁₀ x 6¹/₁₀in)
Fabric	28-count Jobelan
Fabric count	14 holes per inch
Stitch	cross stitch
Stitch count	59 x 85
Stitch size	worked over 2 threads
Number of strands	2

Materials required

 Anchor: 101

Anchor Lamé: 300*

De Haviland: purple

Anchor Lamé: 303* **

*Use 4 strands

**Backstitch

DIWALI MEHNDI CARD

RANGOLI CARD 1

Design size	8.2 x 8.2cm (3³⁄₁₀ x 3³⁄₁₀in)
Fabric	Airforce blue 28-count Jobelan
Fabric count	14 holes per inch
Stitch	cross stitch
Stitch count	45 x 45
Stitch size	worked over 2 threads
Number of strands	1

Materials required

■ Anchor Perlé 8: 386
■ Mill Hill Glass Seed beads: 00123 x 59

RANGOLI CARD 2

Design size	7.4 x 7.4cm (2⁹⁄₁₀ x 2⁹⁄₁₀in)
Fabric	Airforce blue 28-count Jobelan
Fabric count	14 holes per inch
Stitch	cross stitch
Stitch count	41 x 41
Stitch size	worked over 2 threads
Number of strands	1

Materials required

■ Anchor Perlé 8: 386
■ Mill Hill Glass Seed beads: 00123 x 12

DIWALI LEAF CARD

Design size	8 x 12cm (3⅒ x 4⅞in)
Fabric	28-count Jobelan
Fabric count	14 holes per inch
Stitch	cross stitch
Stitch count	44 x 66
Stitch size	worked on over 2 threads
Number of strands	2

Materials required

▇ Anchor: 1325

EID CARDS

Ramadan celebrates the month in the Islamic year during which an angel spoke to Muhammed. As Muslims follow Muhammed's teaching throughout their lives, it is of great importance to them.

Ramadan is a time of self-discipline, when Muslims eat nothing between sunrise and sunset. At the end of Ramadan, on Eid-ul-Fitr, the first day of the new month, celebrations take place. Gifts of sugared almonds, sweets and nuts are given and Eid cards are exchanged. These usually open in the opposite way to Western cards and are decorated with wonderful Islamic patterns.

I have used three such designs here, which, as well as being appropriate for Eid-ul-Fitr, can be made up to open either way, and used for any other occasion. I fastened two blue beads and six blue and silver tubes onto a silver shisha ring, then glued it to the bottom of the 'Circles in blue' design to finish it off.

Card details:

Blue and silver card	Dark blue, oval aperture 15.2 x 1.08cm (6 x ⁷⁄₁₀in)
Pink and green card	Dark green, oval aperture 13.5 x 9cm (5³⁄₁₀ x 3½in)
Circles in blue card	Silver, circular aperture 9.5cm (3⁷⁄₁₀in)

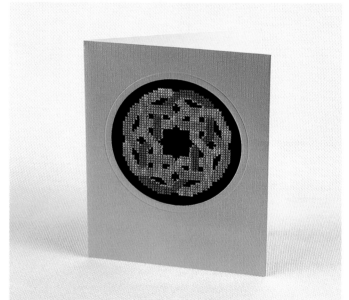

BLUE AND SILVER CARD

Design size	10.7 x 12.2cm (4³⁄₁₀ x 4⁸⁄₁₀in)
Fabric	28-count Jobelan
Fabric count	14 holes per inch
Stitch	cross stitch
Stitch count	59 x 67
Stitch size	worked over 2 threads
Number of strands	2

Materials requried

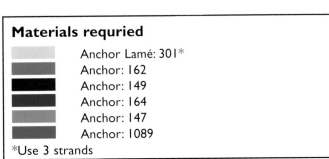

	Anchor Lamé: 301*
	Anchor: 162
	Anchor: 149
	Anchor: 164
	Anchor: 147
	Anchor: 1089

*Use 3 strands

GREEN AND PINK CARD

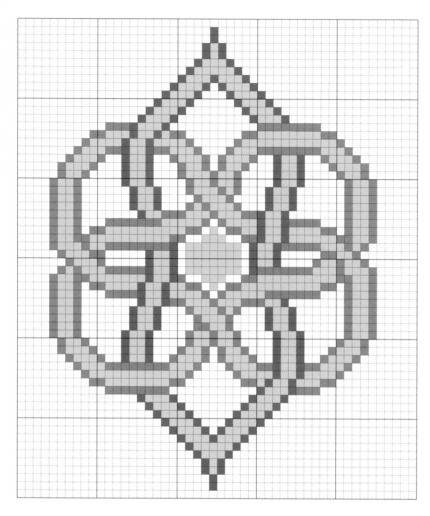

Design size	7.4 x 10.5cm (2⁹⁄₁₀ x 4¹⁄₁₀in)
Fabric	28-count Jobelan
Fabric count	14 holes per inch
Stitch	cross stitch
Stitch count	41 x 58
Stitch size	worked over 2 threads
Number of strands	2

Materials required

	Anchor: 877
	Anchor: 1335 or
	De Haviland green/pink variegated
	Anchor: 1023

CIRCLES IN BLUE

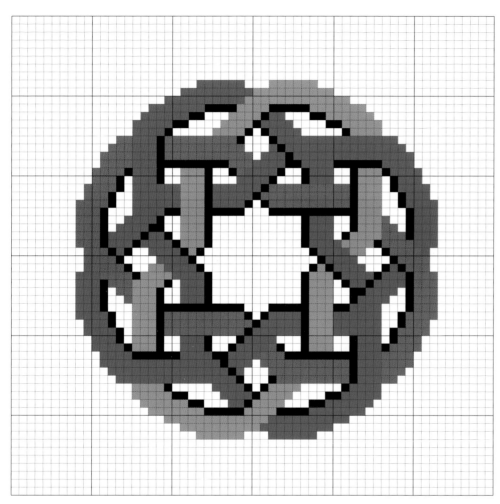

Design size	8.2 x 8.2cm (3³⁄₁₀ x 3³⁄₁₀in)
Fabric	28-count black Jobelan
Fabric count	14 holes per inch
Stitch	cross stitch
Stitch count	45 x 45
Stitch size	worked on over 2 threads
Number of strands	2

Materials required	
▨	Anchor: 1072
▨	Anchor: 146
■	Anchor Lamé: 301*
▨	Anchor: 1345
*Use three strands	

CHINESE NEW YEAR CARDS AND GIFT TAG

The lively blue dragon would be a very appropriate card to send in celebration of this event, but it would also make a striking card for other occasions. The dainty bookmark card and gift tag of Chinese peonies, using some of the same blue threads, would make lovely gifts for anyone who likes pretty things.

Card details:

Dragon card	Dark blue, oval aperture 13.3 x 8.9cm (5³⁄₁₀ x 3½in)
Bookmark card	Cream, aperture 13.5 x 3.1cm (5³⁄₁₀ x 1³⁄₁₀in)
Peony gift tag	Cream, circular aperture 4cm (1½in)

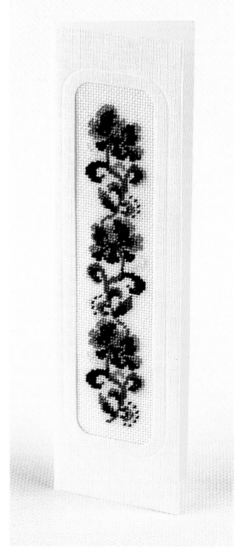

CHINESE DRAGON CARD

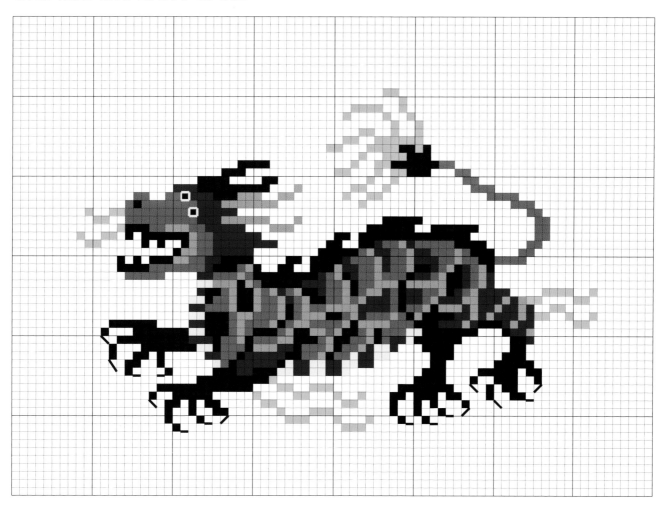

Design size	11.8 x 7.8cm (4⁹⁄₁₀ x 3¹⁄₁₀in)
Fabric	28-count Jobelan
Fabric count	14 holes per inch
Stitch	cross stitch
Stitch count	65 x 43
Stitch size	worked over 2 threads
Number of strands	2

Materials required

- Anchor: 152
- Anchor: 149
- Anchor: 147
- Anchor: 145
- Anchor: 386
- Anchor Lamé: 303*/Stranded cotton 298
- Anchor: 386 (Eyes)**
- Anchor: 152 (Claws)**

*Use 4 strands
**Backstitch

CHINESE PEONY BOOKMARK CARD

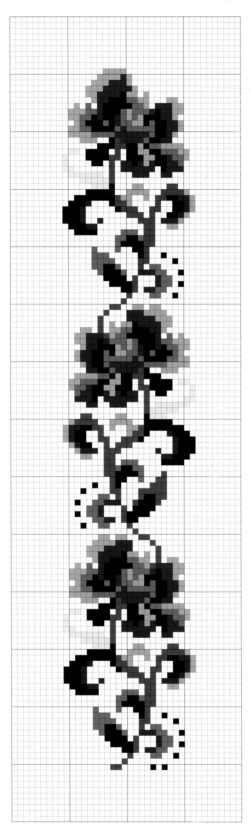

Design size	2.7 x 14.1cm (1 x 5½in)
Fabric count	22 holes per inch
Stitch	half-cross
Stitch count	23 x 122
Stitch size	worked over every thread
Number of strands	2

Materials required

■	Anchor: 152
■	Anchor: 149
■	Anchor: 147/140
■	Anchor: 145
□	Anchor Perlé 8: 386
■	Anchor: 245

CHINESE PEONY GIFT TAG

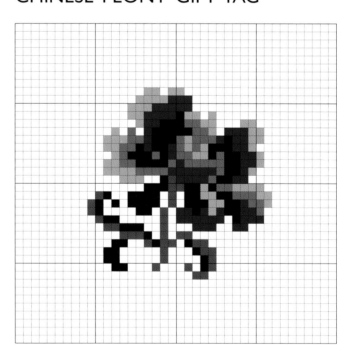

Design size	2.7 x 2.8cm (1 x 1⅛in)
Fabric count	22 holes per inch
Stitch	half-cross
Stitch count	23 x 24
Stitch size	worked over every thread
Number of strands	2

CHRISTMAS CARDS AND GIFT TAGS

Christmas is a time for sending cards, and these special cards and gift tags are sure to bring pleasure to friends and relatives. I have included six cards and gift tags and, in addition to the threads, have used red, green and silver cards, bows and ribbon to give a festive feel to the set. The Christmas rose, without the silver bow, would also make a lovely birthday card.

Card details:

Christmas rose card	White, oval aperture 8.6 x 6.4cm ($3\frac{4}{10}$ x $2\frac{1}{2}$in)
Bells card	White, oval aperture 8.6 x 6.4cm ($3\frac{4}{10}$ x $2\frac{1}{2}$in)
Christmas windows	Silver, (4x) 5.3 x 3.2cm ($2\frac{1}{10}$ x $1\frac{3}{10}$in)
Wreath card	Silver, circular aperture 8.3cm ($3\frac{3}{10}$in)
Yew/bow card	White, circular aperture 8.3cm ($3\frac{3}{10}$in) in square card
Holly card	Silver, circular aperture 8.3cm ($3\frac{3}{10}$in)
Holly gift tag	Silver, circular aperture 4cm ($1\frac{1}{2}$in)
Other gift tags	White, circular aperture 4cm ($1\frac{1}{2}$in)

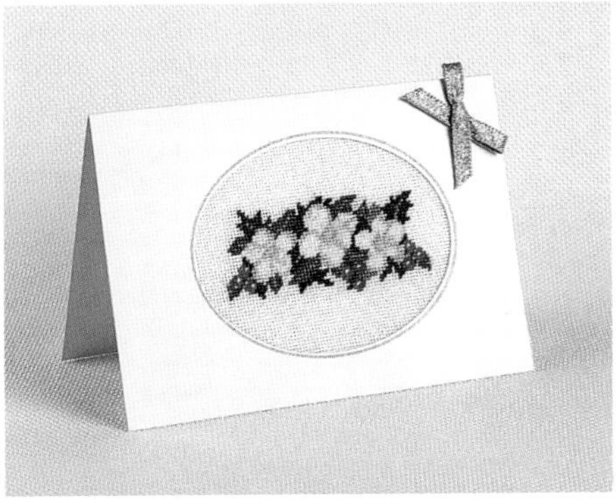

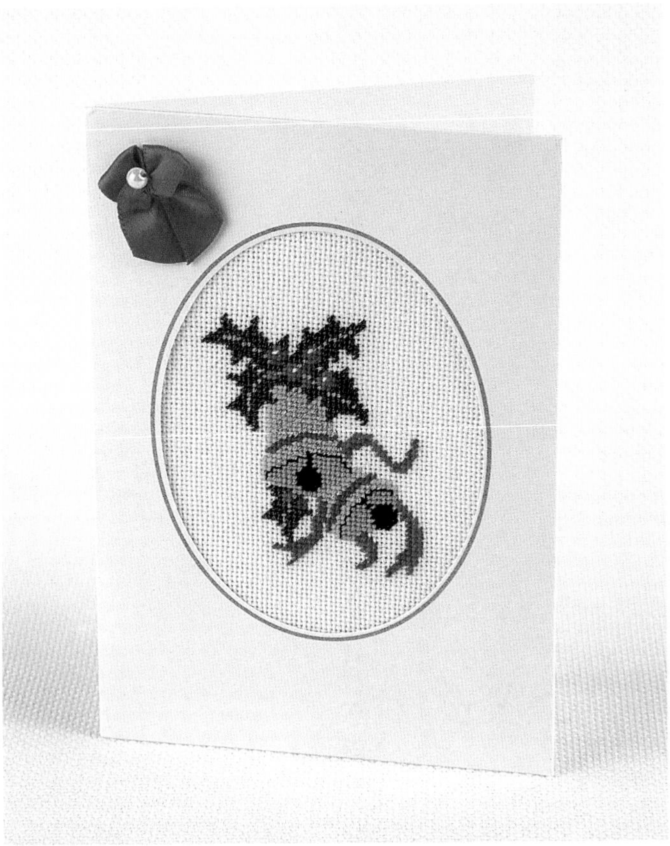

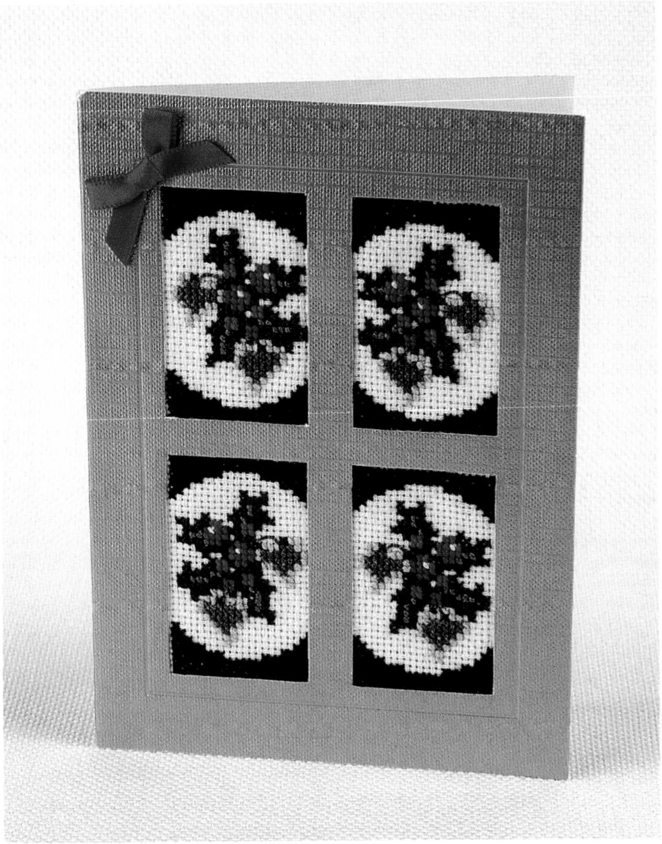

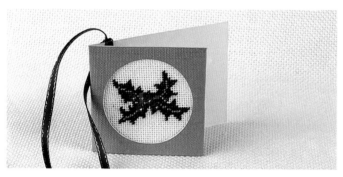

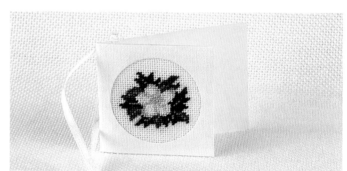

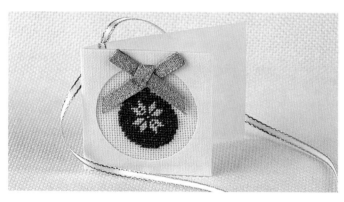

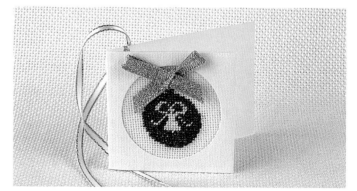

CHRISTMAS ROSE CARD

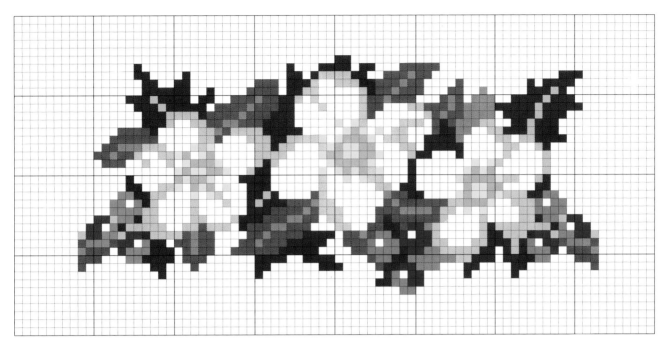

Design size	7.5 x 3.5cm (3 x 1⅜in)
Fabric count	22 holes per inch
Stitch	half-cross
Stitch count	65 x 30
Stitch size	worked over every thread
Number of strands	2

Materials required

	Anchor: 268
	Anchor: 266
	Anchor: 269
	Anchor: 280
	Anchor: 289
	Anchor: 13
	Anchor: 1
	Anchor: 397
	Anchor: 254
	Anchor: 334

CHRISTMAS ROSE GIFT TAG

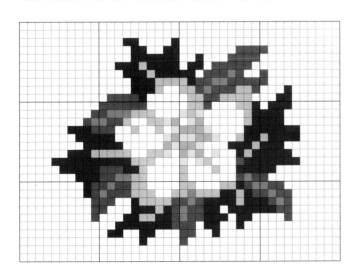

Design size	3.1 x 2.5cm (1⅜ x 1in)
Fabric count	26 holes per inch
Stitch	half-cross
Stitch count	32 x 26
Stitch size	worked over every thread
Number of strands	2

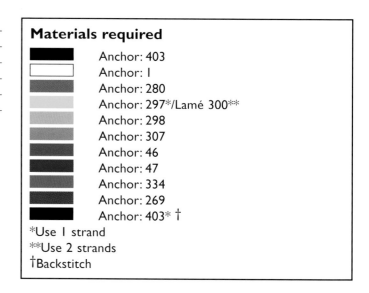

CHRISTMAS BELLS CARD

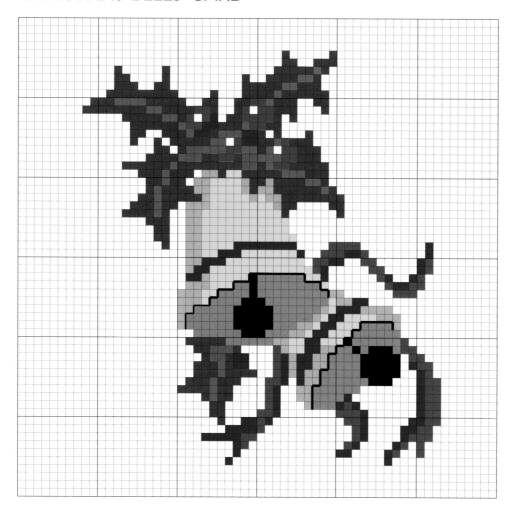

Design size	5.2 x 6cm (2 x 2⅜in)
Fabric count	22 holes per inch
Stitch	half-cross
Stitch count	45 x 52
Stitch size	worked over every thread
Number of strands	2

Materials required

⬛	Anchor: 403
⬜	Anchor: 1
▨	Anchor: 280
▨	Anchor: 297*/Lamé 300**
▨	Anchor: 298
▨	Anchor: 307
▨	Anchor: 46
▨	Anchor: 47
▨	Anchor: 334
▨	Anchor: 269
⬛	Anchor: 403* †

*Use 1 strand
**Use 2 strands
†Backstitch

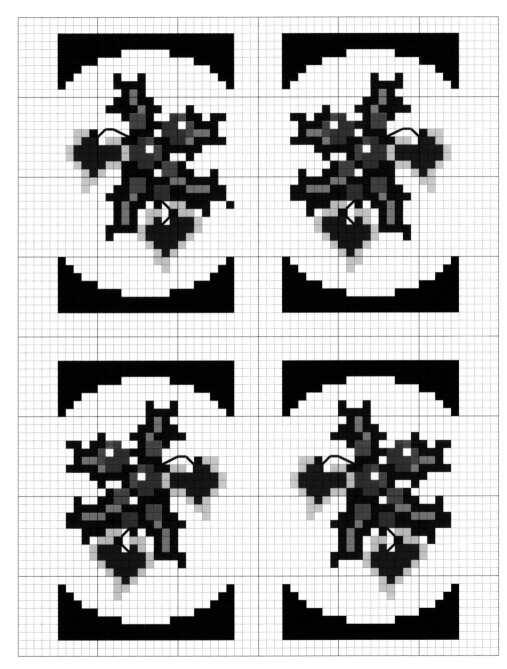

WINDOWS CARD

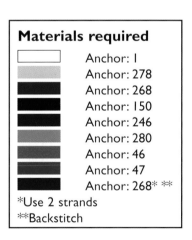

Materials required

	Anchor: 1
	Anchor: 278
	Anchor: 268
	Anchor: 150
	Anchor: 246
	Anchor: 280
	Anchor: 46
	Anchor: 47
	Anchor: 268* **

*Use 2 strands
**Backstitch

Design size	7.9 x 12.1cm (3¹/₁₀ x 4⁵/₁₀in)
Fabric count	16 holes per inch
Stitch	cross stitch
Stitch count	50 x 76
Stitch size	worked over every thread
Number of strands	2

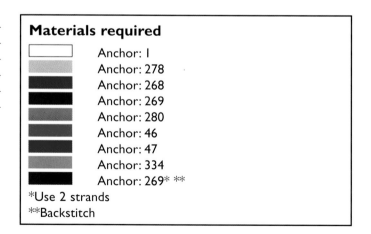

WREATH CARD

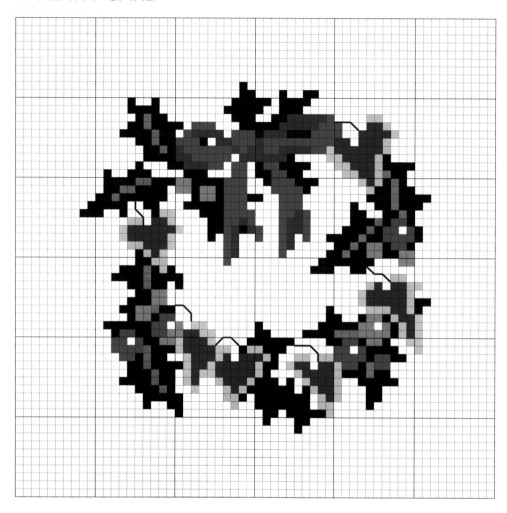

Design size	7 x 7cm (2⁹⁄₁₀ x 2⁹⁄₁₀in)
Fabric count	16 holes per inch
Stitch	cross stitch
Stitch count	44 x 44
Stitch size	worked over every thread
Number of strands	2

Materials required

	Anchor: 1
	Anchor: 278
	Anchor: 268
	Anchor: 269
	Anchor: 280
	Anchor: 46
	Anchor: 47
	Anchor: 334
	Anchor: 269* **

*Use 2 strands
**Backstitch

YEW BOW CARD

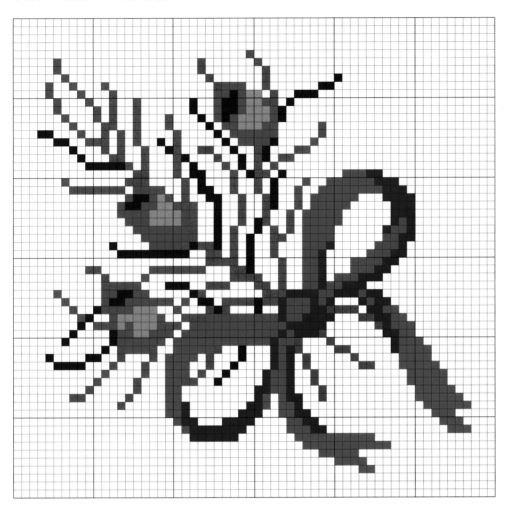

Design size	5.3 x 5.2cm (2¹⁄₁₀ x 2in)
Fabric count	26 holes per inch
Stitch	half-cross
Stitch count	54 x 53
Stitch size	worked over every thread
Number of strands	2

Materials required

	Anchor: 266
	Anchor: 266/268
	Anchor: 358
	Anchor: 46
	Anchor: 47
	Anchor: 334

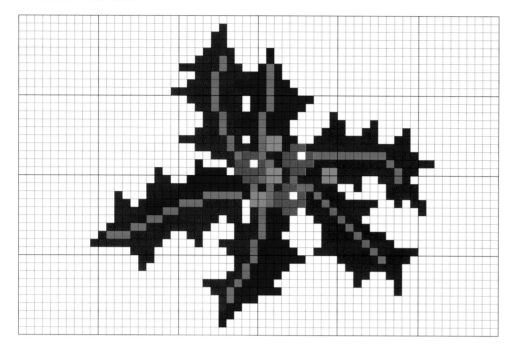

HOLLY CARD

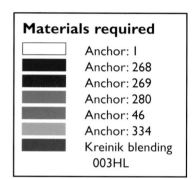

Materials required	
☐	Anchor: 1
■	Anchor: 268
■	Anchor: 269
■	Anchor: 280
■	Anchor: 46
■	Anchor: 334
■	Kreinik blending 003HL

Design size	6.8 x 6cm (2⁷⁄₁₀ x 2⁴⁄₁₀in)
Fabric count	16 holes per inch
Stitch	cross stitch
Stitch count	43 x 38
Stitch size	worked over every thread
Number of strands	2

HOLLY GIFT TAG

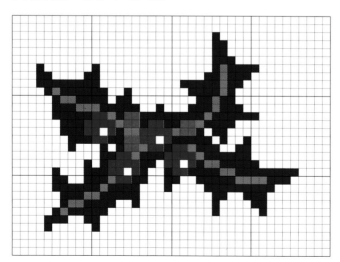

Design size	3.2 x 2.4cm (1³⁄₁₀ x 1in)
Fabric count	26 holes per inch
Stitch	half-cross
Stitch count	33 x 25
Stitch size	worked over every thread
Number of strands	2

RED BAUBLE GIFT TAG

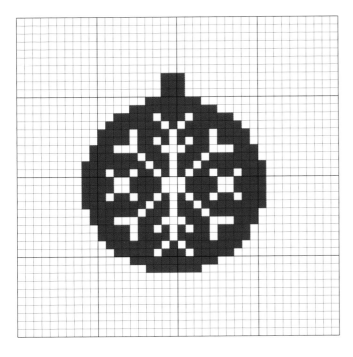

Design size	2.2 x 2.4cm (⅞ x 1in)
Fabric count	26 holes per inch
Stitch	half-cross
Stitch count	23 x 25
Stitch size	worked over every thread
Number of strands	2

Materials required

☐	Anchor: 1
■	Anchor: 47/Kreinik blending 003HL

TURQUOISE BAUBLE GIFT TAG

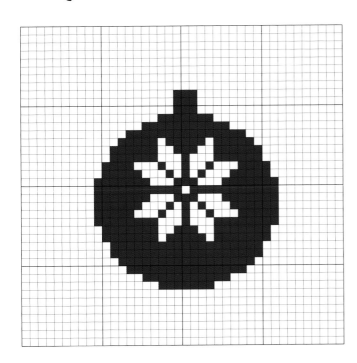

Design size	2.2 x 2.4cm (⅞ x 1in)
Fabric count	26 holes per inch
Stitch	half-cross
Stitch count	23 x 25
Stitch size	worked over every thread
Number of strands	2

Materials required

☐	Anchor: 1
■	Anchor: 188/Kreinik blending 029

BRIGHT GREEN BAUBLE GIFT TAG

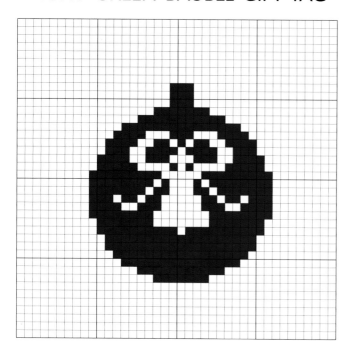

Design size	2.2 x 2.4cm (⅞ x 1in)
Fabric count	26 holes per inch
Stitch	half-cross
Stitch count	23 x 25
Stitch size	worked over every thread
Number of strands	2

Materials required

☐	Anchor: 1
■	Anchor: 228/Kreinik blending 008HL 326

DARK GREEN BAUBLE GIFT TAG

Design size	2.4 x 2.7cm (1 x 1⅒in)
Fabric count	26 holes per inch
Stitch	half-cross
Stitch count	25 x 28
Stitch size	worked over every thread
Number of strands	2

Materials required

☐	Anchor: 1
■	Anchor: 269/Kreinik blending 015HL 406
☐	Anchor: 1 (Candle)*

*Backstitch

ANNIVERSARY CARDS AND GIFT TAGS

Anniversaries are definitely occasions for celebration. I have designed two cards which can easily be adapted to be appropriate for any anniversary and also sent as general cards. I have given the alternative thread colours for Golden, Ruby and Silver Anniversaries, but for birthdays or cards of thanks, any dark, medium and light tones of pinks or soft oranges or yellows may be substituted. The little rosebud, when stitched on 22-count fabric, makes a lovely gift tag. Other designs, which would be particularly suitable for anniversaries are the Imari vase card on page 104 and the hollyhock card on page 69.

Card details:

Pink rosebud card	Cream, circular aperture 7cm (2⅞in) 18-count
Ruby rosebud card	White, circular aperture 7cm (2⅞in) 16-count
Golden 'E.N' card	Dark green, oval aperture 9 x 13.5cm (3½ x 5⅜in) 14-count
Ruby 'A.C' card	Cream, oval aperture 13.9 x 9.5cm (5½ x 3⅞in) 14-count
Pink rose card	Soft green, oval aperture 10.2 x 7.9cm (4 x 3⅛in) 16-count
Rosebud gift tag	White, circular aperture 4cm (1½in) 22-count

Alternative colours for different anniversaries

	Ruby	Silver	Gold
Dark	305/293	22	Anchor Lamé 301
Medium	293	19/20	397
Light	292	19	1/397

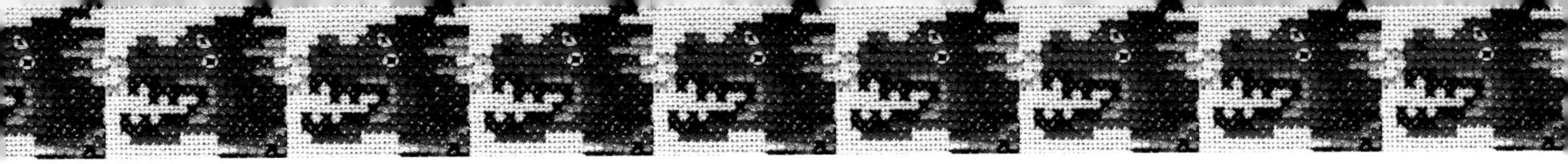

ANNIVERSARY ROSE CARD

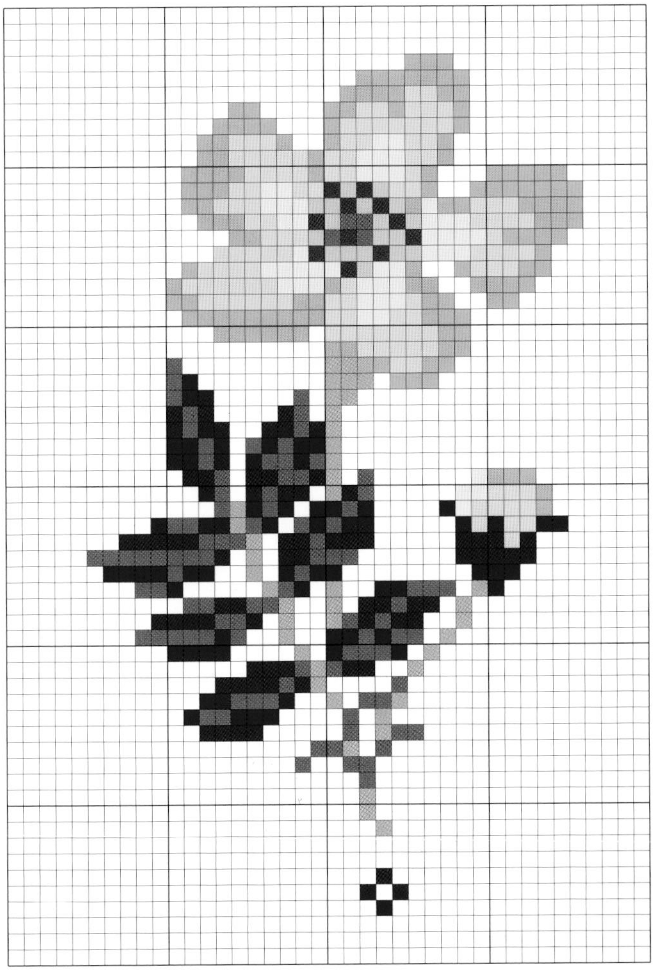

Design size	4.9 x 8.6cm (1 9/10 x 3 4/10in)
Fabric count	16 holes per inch
Stitch	cross stitch
Stitch count	31 x 54
Stitch size	worked over every thread
Number of strands	2

Materials required

- Anchor: 264
- Anchor: 266
- Anchor: 266/268
- Anchor: 352
- Anchor: 305
- Anchor: 293 (Medium)
- Anchor: 292 (Light)
- Anchor: 305/293

ANNIVERSARY ROSE GIFT TAG

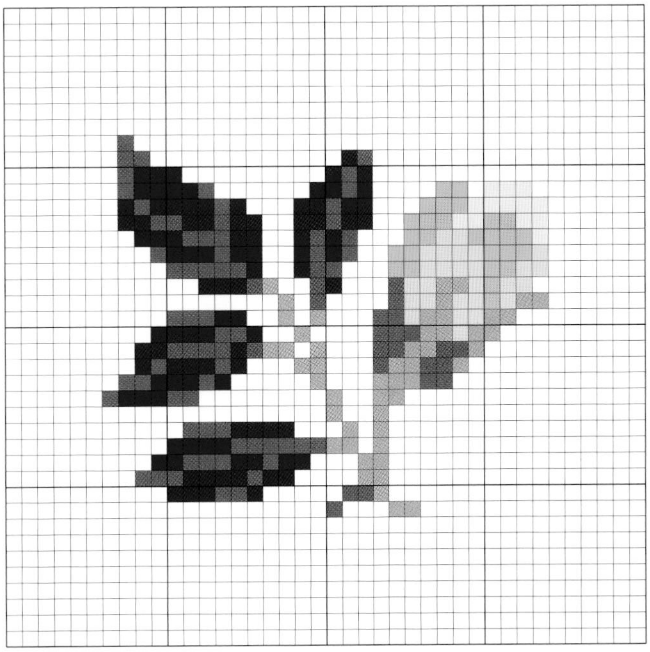

Design size	3.2 x 2.8cm (1 3/10 x 1 1/10in)
Fabric count	22 holes per inch
Stitch	cross stitch
Stitch count	28 x 24
Stitch size	worked over every thread
Number of strands	2

FLOWERS AND FRUITS

POPPIES CARD, BOOKMARK CARD AND GIFT TAGS

Poppies are one of my favourite flowers, both wild field poppies and the glorious oriental ones. I have devised a collection of field poppy designs that I am sure will be useful. As they use the same colours of thread, one skein of each colour will stitch a number of cards. The smaller gift tag designs could also be stitched repeatedly up a bookmark card.

Card details:

Card	Snow white, circular aperture 8.3cm (3⅕in)
Bookmark card	Green, aperture size 13.5 x 3.1cm (5⅗ x 1⅕in)
Gift tags	Red, circular aperture 4cm (1½in)

POPPY CARD

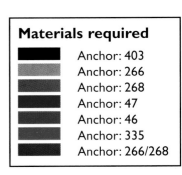

Materials required

⬛	Anchor: 403
▨	Anchor: 266
▨	Anchor: 268
▨	Anchor: 47
▨	Anchor: 46
▨	Anchor: 335
▨	Anchor: 266/268

Design size	6.7 x 6.9cm (2⅗ x 2⁷⁄₁₀in)	Stitch count	58 x 60
Fabric count	22 holes per inch	Stitch size	worked over every thread
Stitch	half-cross	Number of strands	2

GIFT TAG 1

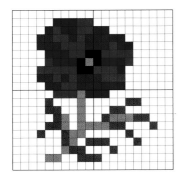

Design size	1.7 x 2.1cm (⁷⁄₁₀ x ⅘in)
Fabric count	22 holes per inch
Stitch	half-cross
Stitch count	15 x 18
Stitch size	worked over every thread
Number of strands	2

POPPY BOOKMARK CARD

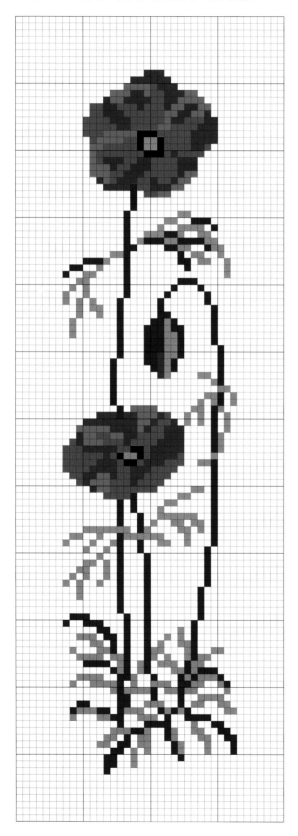

Design size	3 x 12.1cm (1²⁄₁₀ x 4⁸⁄₁₀in)
Fabric count	26 holes per inch
Stitch	half-cross
Stitch count	26 x 105
Stitch size	worked over every thread
Number of strands	2

GIFT TAG 2

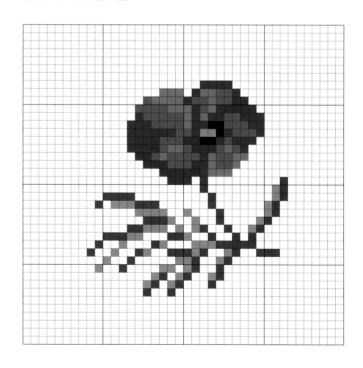

Design size	2.9 x 3.1cm (1¹⁄₁₀ x 1³⁄₁₀in)
Fabric count	22 holes per inch
Stitch	half-cross
Stitch count	25 x 27
Stitch size	worked over every thread
Number of strands	2

WILD ROSE AND ROSEHIPS BOOKMARK CARD, CARDS AND GIFT TAGS

T he wild rose is another popular, attractive flower for stitching. This is a varied collection of wild roses and hips, suitable for many occasions. There is room on the large rosehip card for a personalized message, and any initial or number could be taken from the samplers to replace the 'P' in the rosehip ring or the 'D' on the bookmark card. These could be useful for those birthday milestones, i.e. 30, 40, 50 etc.!

Card details:

Rosehip card	White, oval aperture 13.9 x 9.5cm (5½ x 3⁷⁄₁₀in)
Octagonal rose card	Natural parchment effect, circular aperture 8.3cm (3³⁄₁₀in)
Rosehip circle card	Snow white, circular aperture 7cm (2⁸⁄₁₀in)
Rose bookmark card	Cream, aperture 13.5 x 3.1cm (5³⁄₁₀ x 1²⁄₁₀in)
Gift tags	White/red, circular aperture 4cm (1½in)

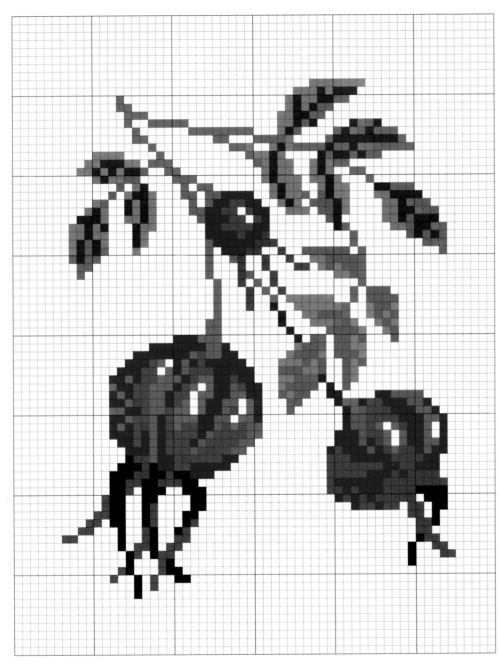

ROSEHIP CARD

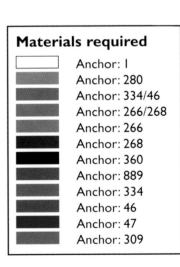

Materials required

	Anchor: 1
	Anchor: 280
	Anchor: 334/46
	Anchor: 266/268
	Anchor: 266
	Anchor: 268
	Anchor: 360
	Anchor: 889
	Anchor: 334
	Anchor: 46
	Anchor: 47
	Anchor: 309

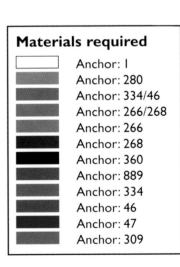

Design size	7.8 x 10.3cm (3 x 4in)
Fabric count	16 holes per inch
Stitch	cross stitch
Stitch count	49 x 65
Stitch size	worked over every thread
Number of strands	2

ROSEHIP CIRCLE CARD

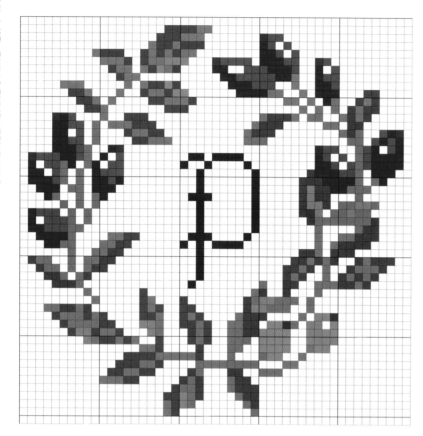

Design size	5.4 x 5.7cm (2¹⁄₁₀ x 2³⁄₁₀in)
Fabric count	22 holes per inch
Stitch	half-cross
Stitch count	47 x 49
Stitch size	worked over every thread
Number of strands	2

Materials required

	Anchor: 1
	Anchor: 266
	Anchor: 268
	Anchor: 369
	Anchor: 905
	Anchor: 46
	Anchor: 47
	Anchor: 20
	Anchor: 369/46

LARGE ROSEHIP GIFT TAG

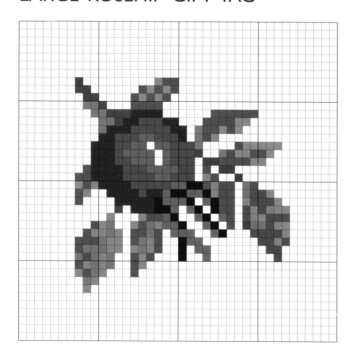

Design size	3.1 x 3.1cm (1³⁄₁₀ x 1³⁄₁₀in)
Fabric count	22 holes per inch
Stitch	half-cross
Stitch count	27 x 27
Stitch size	worked over every thread
Number of strands	2

Materials required

	Anchor: 1
	Anchor: 280
	Anchor: 266
	Anchor: 268
	Anchor: 360
	Anchor: 889
	Anchor: 334
	Anchor: 46
	Anchor: 47
	Anchor: 309

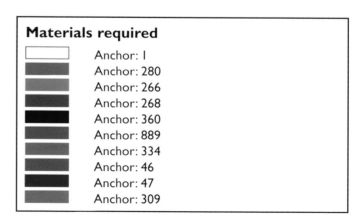

OCTAGONAL ROSE CARD

Design size	7 x 7cm (2⅝ x 2⅝in)
Fabric count	26 holes per inch
Stitch	half-cross
Stitch count	72 x 72
Stitch size	worked over every thread
Number of strands	2

Materials required

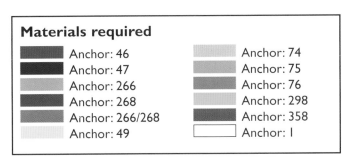

Anchor: 46	Anchor: 74
Anchor: 47	Anchor: 75
Anchor: 266	Anchor: 76
Anchor: 268	Anchor: 298
Anchor: 266/268	Anchor: 358
Anchor: 49	Anchor: 1

ROSE BOOKMARK CARD

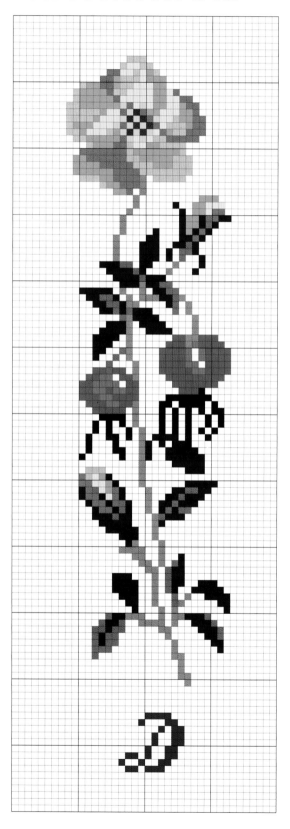

Design size	2.9 x 12.5cm (1⅒ x 4⅞in)
Fabric count	22 holes per inch
Stitch	half-cross
Stitch count	25 x 108
Stitch size	worked over every thread
Number of strands	2

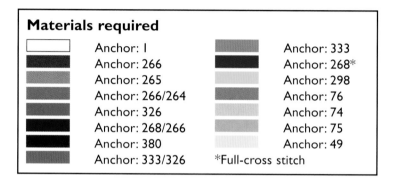

Materials required

	Anchor: I		Anchor: 333
	Anchor: 266		Anchor: 268*
	Anchor: 265		Anchor: 298
	Anchor: 266/264		Anchor: 76
	Anchor: 326		Anchor: 74
	Anchor: 268/266		Anchor: 75
	Anchor: 380		Anchor: 49
	Anchor: 333/326	*Full-cross stitch	

SMALL ROSEHIP GIFT TAG

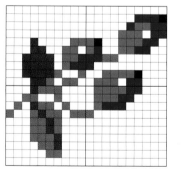

Materials required

	Anchor: I
	Anchor: 266
	Anchor: 268
	Anchor: 889
	Anchor: 334
	Anchor: 47

Design size	2.3 x 2.1cm (⅘ x ⅚in)
Fabric count	22 holes per inch
Stitch	cross stitch
Stitch count	20 x 18
Stitch size	worked over every thread
Number of strands	2

NASTURTIUM CARD AND GIFT TAG

The variety of vivid oranges and reds on these summer flowers give a splash of colour in the garden for months – and they are so easy to grow! Nasturtiums also make an attractive subject for a card, and in this design there is enough space at the bottom left or at the top for 'Thank you', 'Happy Birthday' or any other message. Use the writing from the centre of the mixed stitch sampler on pages 144–147. The silver on the gift tag matches well with the silver line on the card.

Card details:

Card	White, oval aperture 8.6 x 6.4cm (3³⁄₁₀ x 2½in)
Gift tag	Silver, circular aperture 4cm (1½in)

NASTURTIUM CARD

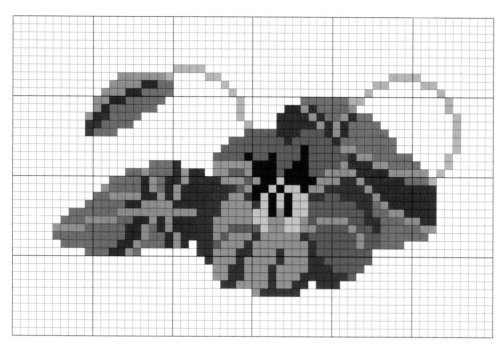

Materials required	
	Anchor: 214
	Anchor: 215
	Anchor: 217
	Anchor: 254
	Anchor: 298
	Anchor: 45
	Anchor: 334
	Anchor: 19
	Anchor: 332
	Anchor: 330

Design size	7.2 x 4.1cm (2⁹⁄₁₀ x 1⁶⁄₁₀in)
Fabric count	18 holes per inch
Stitch	cross stitch
Stitch count	51 x 29
Stitch size	worked over every thread
Number of strands	2

NASTURTIUM GIFT TAG

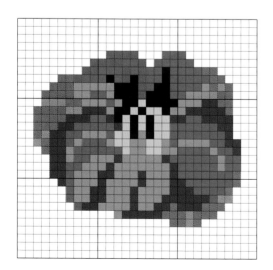

Design size	3 x 2.5cm (1²⁄₁₀ x 1in)
Fabric count	22 holes per inch
Stitch	half-cross
Stitch count	26 x 22
Stitch size	worked over every thread
Number of strands	2

PINKS CARD AND GIFT TAG

This is a very pretty design, which would make a lovely wedding card when finished with a beaded bow like the one here. It is a delicate card, and one that is fairly quick to stitch. I think the touch of silver in this card from Framecraft adds to the celebratory feel.

Card details:

Card	White, oval aperture 13.9 x 9.5cm (5½ x 3⁷⁄₁₀in)
Gift tag	White, circular aperture 4cm (1½in)

PINKS GIFT TAG

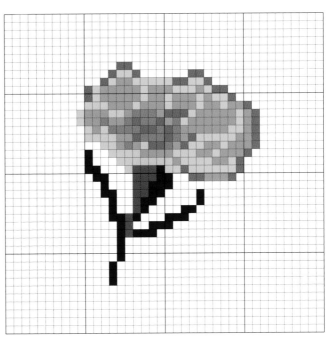

Design size	2.7 x 3.2cm (1 x 1¹⁄₁₀in)
Fabric count	22 holes per inch
Stitch	half-cross
Stitch count	23 x 28
Stitch size	worked over every thread
Number of strands	2

PINKS CARD

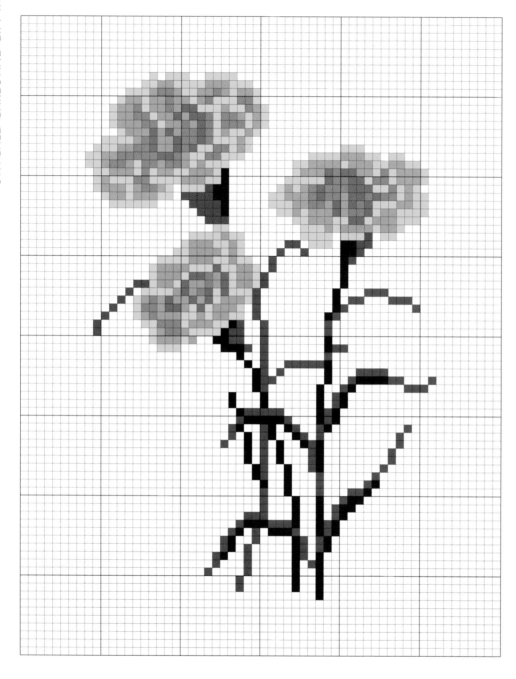

Design size	7 x 10.5cm (2⁹⁄₁₀ x 4¹⁄₁₀in)
Fabric count	16 holes per inch
Stitch	cross stitch
Stitch count	44 x 66
Stitch size	worked over every thread
Number of strands	2

Materials required

	Anchor: 1023
	Anchor: 1021
	Anchor: 1021/1023
	Anchor: 1023/1025
	Anchor: 216
	Anchor: 215

BLUE DAISY CARD, BOOKMARK CARD AND GIFT TAG

This is a fun set because, although I love the daisy shape, a white daisy wasn't going to be bright enough for the card that I had in mind, so I used the shape but chose some pretty turquoise colours and it worked very successfully.

I took two of the individual daisies from the bookmark card and stitched them on 22-count fabric to make a card and gift tag.

Card details

Card	White, square aperture 4cm (1½in)
Bookmark card	White, aperture 13.5 x 3.1cm (5³⁄₁₀ x 1³⁄₁₀in)
Gift tag	White, circular aperture 3cm (1³⁄₁₀in)

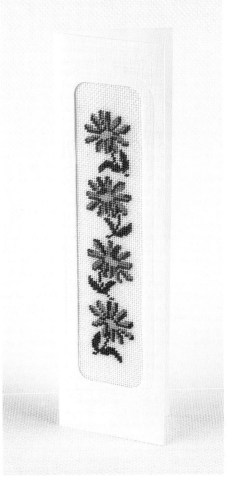

BLUE DAISY BOOKMARK CARD

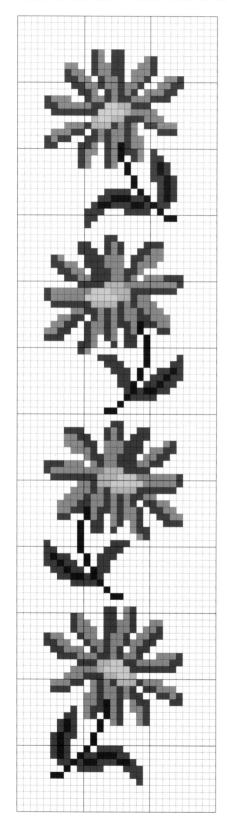

Design size	2.4 x 12.8cm (1 x 5in)
Fabric count	22 holes per inch
Stitch	half-cross
Stitch count	21 x 111
Stitch size	worked over every thread
Number of strands	2

Materials required

	Anchor: 297
	Anchor: 298
	Anchor: 186
	Anchor: 188
	Anchor: 189

BEADED HOLLYHOCK CARD

This is a bright and cheerful card, suitable for many occasions but would be particularly apt for an anniversary. Stitch the beads on last, using a single strand of thread and a half-cross stitch. In each case, define the individual petals with a metallic thread of the appropriate colour.

Ruby   Substitute 22, 20 and 19 for 54, 52 and 50
Golden   Substitute 305, 293 and 292 for 54, 52 and 50
Silver   Substitute 397, 01 and white Marlitt thread for
                54, 52 and 50 and work on a pale blue fabric

Card details:
Dark green, rectangular aperture 13.5 x 9cm (5³⁄₁₀ x 3½in)

BEADED HOLLYHOCK CARD

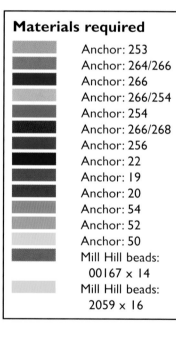

Materials required

Anchor: 253
Anchor: 264/266
Anchor: 266
Anchor: 266/254
Anchor: 254
Anchor: 266/268
Anchor: 256
Anchor: 22
Anchor: 19
Anchor: 20
Anchor: 54
Anchor: 52
Anchor: 50
Mill Hill beads:
   00167 x 14
Mill Hill beads:
   2059 x 16

Design size	7 x 12.4cm (2⅞ x 4⅞in)
Fabric count	16 holes per inch
Stitch	cross stitch
Stitch count	44 x 78
Stitch size	worked over every thread
Number of strands	2

PANSY CARD AND GIFT TAG

Each time I look at this card and gift tag Mother's Day springs to mind, although they would certainly be suitable for other special times. There is not too much stitching in the card, and it would also look attractive stitched on a 14-count fabric and inserted into a larger card. I think the mauve beaded bow and cream card adds a degree of importance and sophistication!

Card details:

Card   Cream, oval aperture 8.6 x 6.4cm (3³⁄₁₀ x 2½in)

Gift tag   Cream, circular aperture 4cm (1½in)

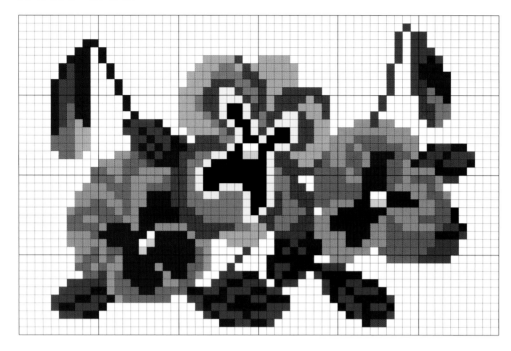

PANSY CARD

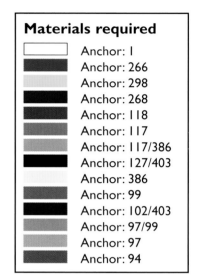

Materials required

	Anchor: 1
	Anchor: 266
	Anchor: 298
	Anchor: 268
	Anchor: 118
	Anchor: 117
	Anchor: 117/386
	Anchor: 127/403
	Anchor: 386
	Anchor: 99
	Anchor: 102/403
	Anchor: 97/99
	Anchor: 97
	Anchor: 94

Design size	6.1 x 4.4cm (2⅜ x 1⅞in)
Fabric count	22 holes per inch
Stitch	half-cross
Stitch count	53 x 38
Stitch size	worked over every thread
Number of strands	2

PANSY GIFT TAG

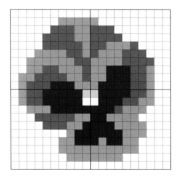

Design size	2 x 2.1cm (⅘ x ⅚in)
Fabric count	22 holes per inch
Stitch	half-cross
Stitch count	17 x 18
Stitch size	worked over every thread
Number of strands	2

LILY CARD

Lilies are one of my favourite flowers, so I wanted to include one in these card designs. On a more sombre note, this could be stitched in white and pale greys with a single strand of dark grey outlining the petals. It would then be suitable for a thoughtful 'sympathy' card.

The long stamens are worked after the stitching is complete, and each one is composed of one long stitch. The 'spots' in stranded cotton could be replaced with beads of a dark colour.

Card details:

Rose Lorenzo parchment effect, oval aperture 10.2 x 7.9cm (4 x 3⅒in)

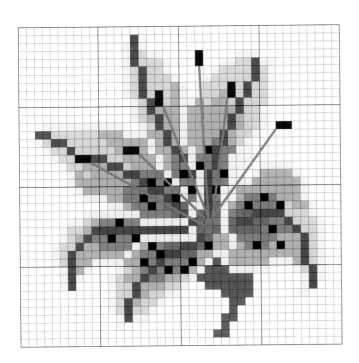

Materials required

	Anchor: 386/49
	Anchor: 403
	Anchor: 49/1
	Anchor: 49/75
	Anchor: 75
	Anchor: 68
	Anchor: 69
	Anchor: 352
	Anchor: 75/68
	Anchor: 268
	Anchor: 843
	Anchor: 843*

*Backstitch

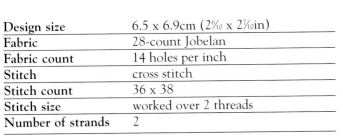

Design size	6.5 x 6.9cm (2⅒ x 2⅞in)
Fabric	28-count Jobelan
Fabric count	14 holes per inch
Stitch	cross stitch
Stitch count	36 x 38
Stitch size	worked over 2 threads
Number of strands	2

JAPONICA INITIAL RING CARD

This bright little design doesn't take very long to stitch, but it is a pretty, personalized card. The central initial could be replaced by a short message. It would make a most acceptable card of thanks.

Card details:

Mellotex white card, circular aperture 8.3cm (3³⁄₁₀in)

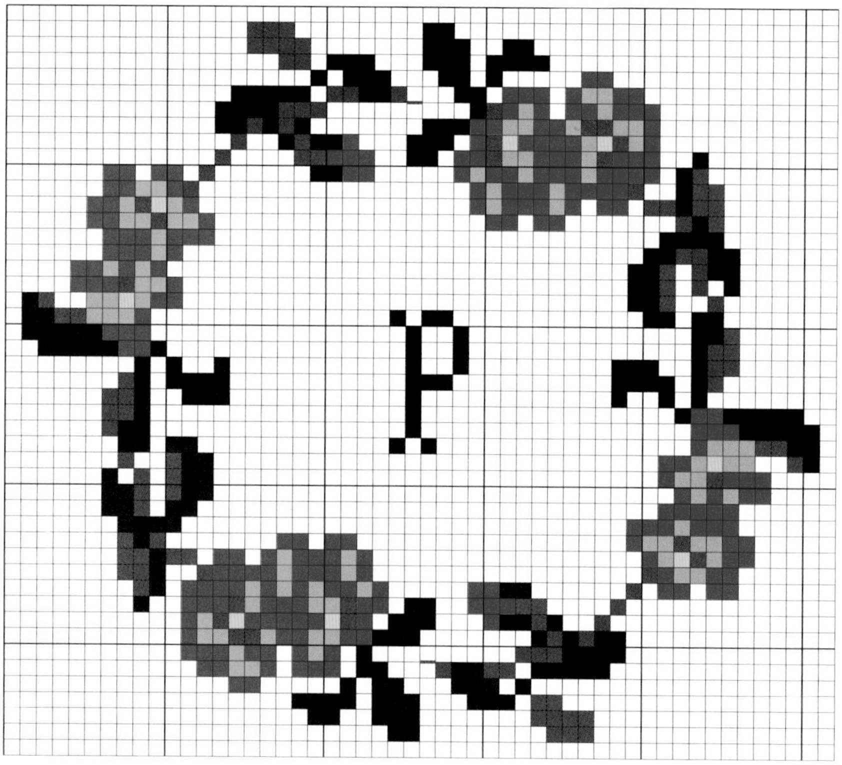

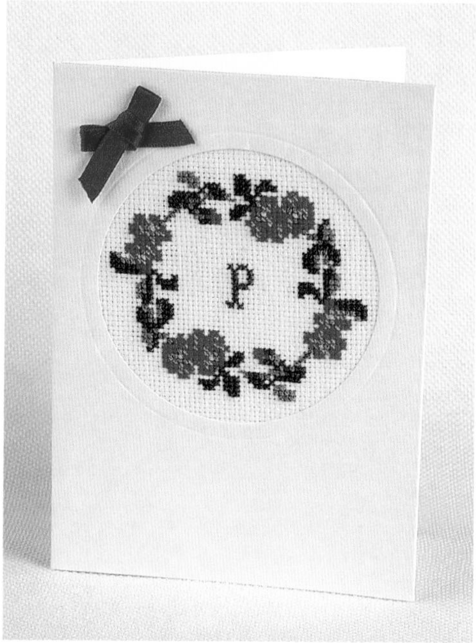

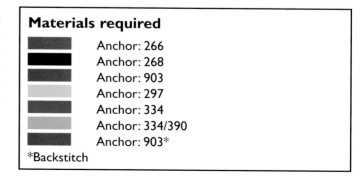

Design size	7.9 x 7.1cm (3¹⁄₁₀ x 2⁸⁄₁₀in)
Fabric count	16 holes per inch
Stitch	cross stitch
Stitch count	50 x 45
Stitch size	worked over every thread
Number of strands	2

Materials required

- Anchor: 266
- Anchor: 268
- Anchor: 903
- Anchor: 297
- Anchor: 334
- Anchor: 334/390
- Anchor: 903*

*Backstitch

ABSTRACT CHINTZ FLOWER CARD AND GIFT TAGS

T his card was adapted from a chintz design, dated 1883. The design would work well in shades of other colours, too, as I have shown with the gift tags.

Card details:

Card	Bright white, oval aperture 10.2 x 7.9cm (4 x 3¹⁄₁₀in)
Gift tags	White/red, circular aperture 4cm (1½in)

ABSTRACT CHINTZ FLOWER GIFT TAG

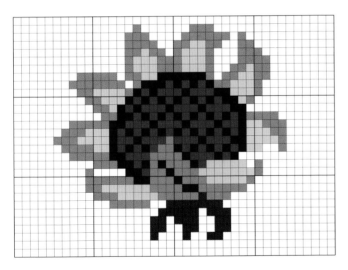

Design size	3.3 x 3.1cm (1³⁄₁₀ x 1²⁄₁₀in)
Fabric count	22 holes per inch
Stitch	half-cross
Stitch count	29 x 27
Stitch size	worked over every thread
Number of strands	2

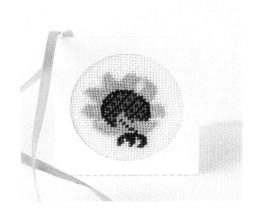

Materials required

■	Anchor: 878
▨	Anchor: 8 (297)
▨	Anchor: 10 (298)
▨	Anchor: 13 (309)
■	Anchor: 45 (359)

*Numbers in brackets are for alternative yellow tones

ABSTRACT CHINTZ FLOWER CARD

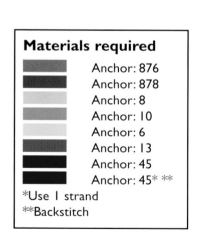

Materials required

	Anchor: 876
	Anchor: 878
	Anchor: 8
	Anchor: 10
	Anchor: 6
	Anchor: 13
	Anchor: 45
	Anchor: 45* **

*Use 1 strand
**Backstitch

Design size	5.4 x 7.9cm (2¹⁄₁₀ x 3¹⁄₁₀in)
Fabric count	22 holes per inch
Stitch	half-cross
Stitch count	47 x 68
Stitch size	worked over every thread
Number of strands	2

BLACKBERRY CARD AND GIFT TAG

I think this is a very simple design, which is quick to work and useful for many occasions. Both cards could easily be stitched in just one evening. The white beads make it particularly distinctive.

Card details:

Card	Snow white, circular aperture 7cm (2⅞in)
Gift tag	White, circular aperture 4cm (1½in)

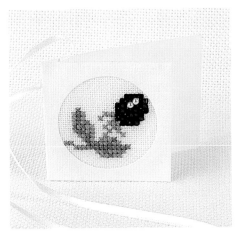

BLACKBERRY CARD

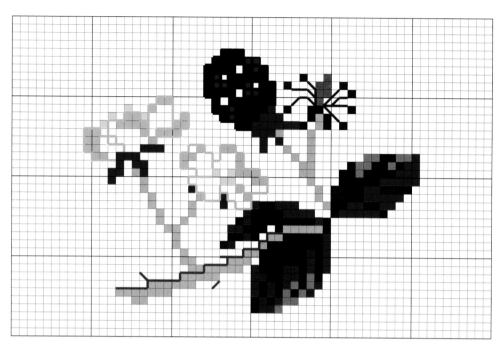

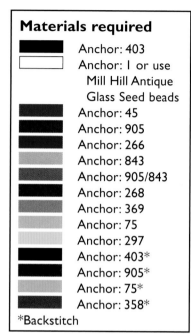

Materials required

■	Anchor: 403
□	Anchor: 1 or use Mill Hill Antique Glass Seed beads
■	Anchor: 45
■	Anchor: 905
■	Anchor: 266
▨	Anchor: 843
▨	Anchor: 905/843
■	Anchor: 268
▨	Anchor: 369
▨	Anchor: 75
▨	Anchor: 297
■	Anchor: 403*
■	Anchor: 905*
▨	Anchor: 75*
▨	Anchor: 358*

*Backstitch

Design size	6.7 x 5.2cm (2⁹⁄₁₀ x 2in)
Fabric count	16 holes per inch
Stitch	cross stitch
Stitch count	42 x 33
Stitch size	worked over every thread
Number of strands	2

BLACKBERRY GIFT TAG

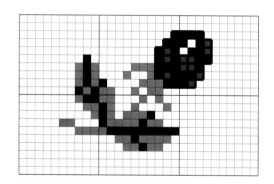

Design size	3.4 x 2.7cm (1³⁄₁₀ x 1in)
Fabric	28-count Jobelan
Fabric count	14 holes per inch
Stitch	cross stitch
Stitch count	19 x 15
Stitch size	worked over 2 threads
Number of strands	2

ORANGES CARD

Some time ago, when I was in Spain, I noticed oranges on the trees in the sunlight and thought what a bright and cheerful card they would make, so here it is! There is room at the top or bottom for a personal message.

Card details:

Snow white, oval aperture 10.2 x 7.9cm (4 x 3¹⁄₁₀in)

Design size	5.6 x 7.6cm (2³⁄₁₀ x 3in)
Fabric count	16 holes per inch
Stitch	cross stitch
Stitch count	35 x 48
Stitch size	worked over every thread
Number of strands	2

Materials required

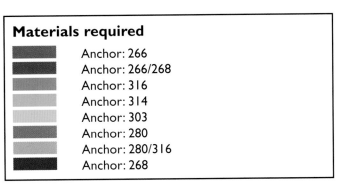

	Anchor: 266
	Anchor: 266/268
	Anchor: 316
	Anchor: 314
	Anchor: 303
	Anchor: 280
	Anchor: 280/316
	Anchor: 268

GARDEN VISITORS
LADYBIRD CARD

This bright little ladybird, stitched in half-cross stitch over every thread on 26-count fabric and then mounted into the small aperture, makes a really unusual card. It could, of course, be stitched in cross stitch on a smaller count fabric and mounted in a larger card, but I think it might then lose some of its charm.

Card details:
White, square aperture 4cm (1½in)

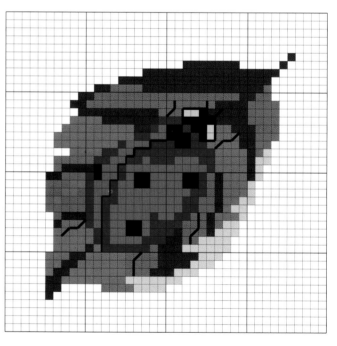

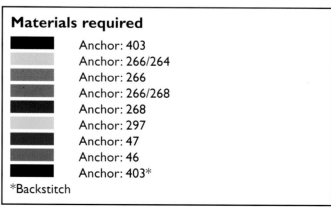

Design size	3 x 3cm (1³⁄₁₀ x 1³⁄₁₀in)
Fabric count	26 holes per inch
Stitch	half-cross
Stitch count	31 x 31
Stitch size	worked over every thread
Number of strands	2

Materials required

▇	Anchor: 403
▨	Anchor: 266/264
▨	Anchor: 266
▨	Anchor: 266/268
▇	Anchor: 268
▨	Anchor: 297
▇	Anchor: 47
▇	Anchor: 46
▇	Anchor: 403*

*Backstitch

DRAGONFLY CARD

I enjoy looking at my pond and am always pleased when a dragonfly visits. It is a such a beautiful creature and makes a striking subject for a stitched card. The bright blue card is particularly effective as it picks out the colour in the dragonfly's tail. The design does not take much time to stitch, and I am sure it would be much appreciated.

Card details:

Cobalt Prisma felt effect, oval aperture 7.6 x 5cm (3 x 2in)

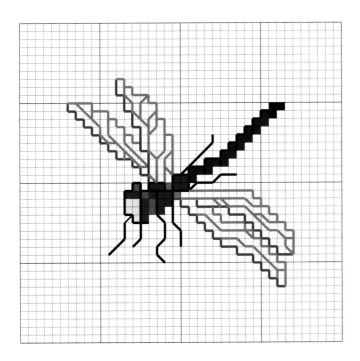

Design size	4.4 x 4.1cm (1⁷⁄₁₀ x 1⁵⁄₈in)
Fabric count	16 holes per inch
Stitch	cross stitch
Stitch count	28 x 26
Stitch size	worked over every thread
Number of strands	2

Materials required

⬛	Anchor: 403
⬛	Anchor: 850
⬛	Anchor: 266
⬛	Anchor: 266/1090
⬛	Anchor: 164
⬜	Anchor: 295/266
⬛	Anchor: 403* **
⬛	Anchor: 850* **
⬛	Anchor: 850* †

*Backstitch **Use 1 strand †Use 2 strands

RED ADMIRAL BUTTERFLY CARDS AND GIFT TAG

Stitched butterflies make lovely gifts, and one of my favourites is the Red Admiral. These butterflies almost appear to be made of velvet when they are flying or resting in the sun. I have designed a collection of them here, using the same colours, and as each one only takes a small amount of thread, oddments can be used up.

Card details:

Red Admiral card	White, oval aperture 13.9 x 9.5cm (5½ x 3⅞in)
Red Admiral and Michaelmas Daisy card	Pale cream, square aperture 5.4cm (2in)
Gift tag	Red, circular aperture 4cm (1½in)

RED ADMIRAL CARD

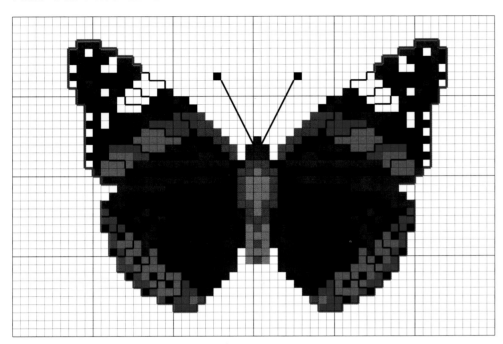

Design size	8.5 x 6.2cm (3¾₀ x 2½in)
Fabric	pale grey 28-count Jobelan
Fabric count	14 holes per inch
Stitch	cross stitch
Stitch count	47 x 34
Stitch size	worked over 2 threads
Number of strands	2

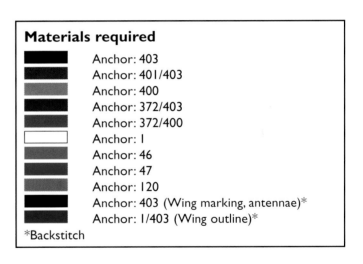

Materials required

⬛	Anchor: 403
⬛	Anchor: 401/403
⬛	Anchor: 400
⬛	Anchor: 372/403
⬛	Anchor: 372/400
⬜	Anchor: 1
⬛	Anchor: 46
⬛	Anchor: 47
⬛	Anchor: 120
⬛	Anchor: 403 (Wing marking, antennae)*
⬛	Anchor: 1/403 (Wing outline)*

*Backstitch

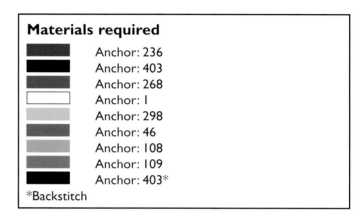

RED ADMIRAL AND MICHAELMAS DAISY CARD

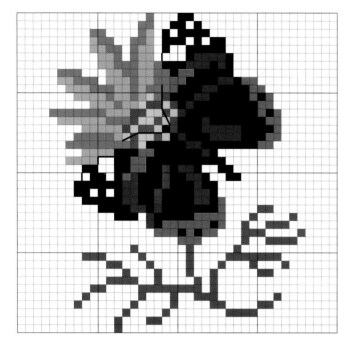

Design size	3.7 x 4.6cm (1½ x 1⅘in)
Fabric count	22 holes per inch
Stitch	half-cross
Stitch count	32 x 40
Stitch size	worked over every thread
Number of strands	2

Materials required

	Anchor: 236
	Anchor: 403
	Anchor: 268
	Anchor: 1
	Anchor: 298
	Anchor: 46
	Anchor: 108
	Anchor: 109
	Anchor: 403*

*Backstitch

RED ADMIRAL GIFT TAG

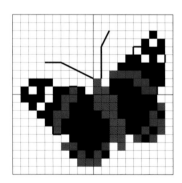

Materials required

	Anchor: 403
	Anchor: 1
	Anchor: 358
	Anchor: 47
	Anchor: 403*

*Backstitch

Design size	2.1 x 2cm (⅞ x ⅞in)
Fabric count	22 holes per inch
Stitch	cross stitch
Stitch count	18 x 17
Stitch size	worked over every thread
Number of strands	2

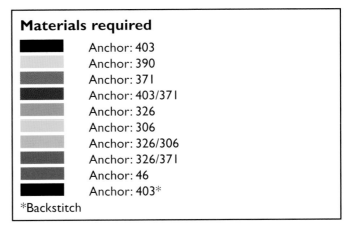

TIGERMOTH CARD

T his garden Tigermoth, so-called because of its tiger-like stripes, is so attractive and brightly coloured that it could easily be mistaken for a butterfly, though it is usually about more at night. The pattern and size of this species of moth are varied and no two are identical. A repeat of the design makes a striking border or bookmark.

Card details:

White Lorenzo parchment effect, circular aperture 7cm (2⅞in)

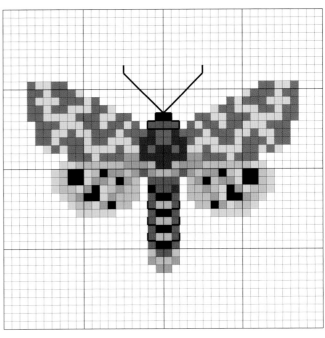

Design size	5.4 x 4.1cm (2⅒ x 1⅗in)
Fabric count	16 holes per inch
Stitch	cross stitch
Stitch count	34 x 26
Stitch size	worked over every thread
Number of strands	2

Materials required

⬛	Anchor: 403
⬜	Anchor: 390
▦	Anchor: 371
▩	Anchor: 403/371
▦	Anchor: 326
▨	Anchor: 306
▨	Anchor: 326/306
▩	Anchor: 326/371
▦	Anchor: 46
⬛	Anchor: 403*

*Backstitch

PEACOCK BUTTERFLY CARD

Peacock butterflies are easily recognized by their rich colours and startling false eyes. I like to see a group of them on the windfall apples and plums. This card, as well as being suitable for a birthday, would make a lovely 'thank you' card. There is room for a message above the design.

Card details:
Light cream, oval aperture 7.6 x 5cm (3 x 2in)

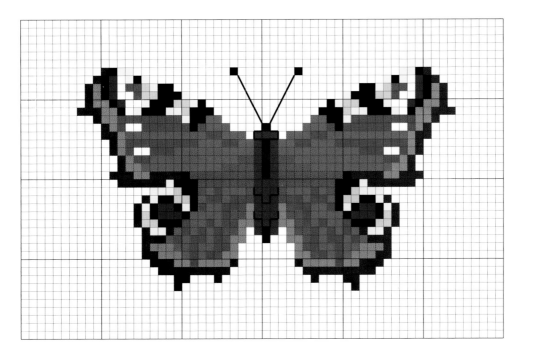

Design size	5.4 x 3.2cm (2¹⁄₁₀ x 1³⁄₁₀in)
Fabric count	22 holes per inch
Stitch	half-cross
Stitch count	47 x 28
Stitch size	worked over every thread
Number of strands	2

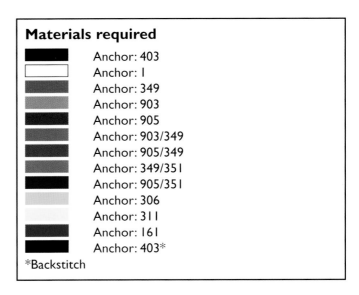

Materials required

	Anchor: 403
	Anchor: 1
	Anchor: 349
	Anchor: 903
	Anchor: 905
	Anchor: 903/349
	Anchor: 905/349
	Anchor: 349/351
	Anchor: 905/351
	Anchor: 306
	Anchor: 311
	Anchor: 161
	Anchor: 403*

*Backstitch

PAINTED LADY BUTTERFLY CARD

These migrant butterflies vary in number from year to year. They arrive during May and June having travelled over 1000km (600 miles), and can be seen gathering nectar from thistles and nettles. Having flown so far, as well as being colourful, I think they are worthy of being represented on a card!

Card details:

White, oval aperture 13.9 x 9.5cm (5½ x 3⁷⁄₁₀in)

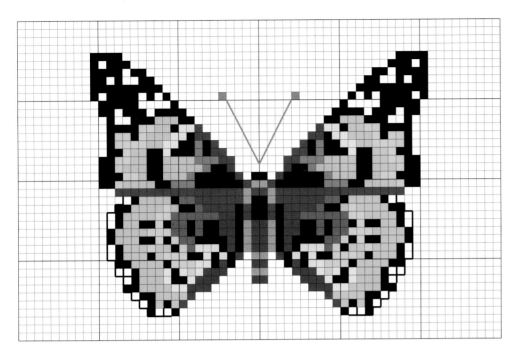

Design size	7.6 x 6cm (3 x 2⅜in)
Fabric	pale grey 28-count Jobelan
Fabric count	14 holes per inch
Stitch	cross stitch
Stitch count	42 x 33
Stitch size	worked over 2 threads
Number of strands	2

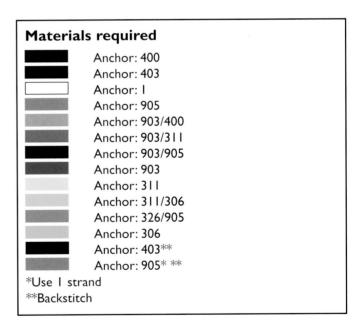

Materials required

	Anchor: 400
	Anchor: 403
	Anchor: 1
	Anchor: 905
	Anchor: 903/400
	Anchor: 903/311
	Anchor: 903/905
	Anchor: 903
	Anchor: 311
	Anchor: 311/306
	Anchor: 326/905
	Anchor: 306
	Anchor: 403**
	Anchor: 905* **

*Use 1 strand
**Backstitch

FIELD MICE CARDS

These two cards show particularly attractive mice and have a bright touch of red in the form of rosehips. They both use the same colouring and are serviceable small designs for many purposes, not just cards.

Card details:

Field mouse card 1   Natural Lorenzo parchment effect, circular aperture 7cm (2⅝in)

Field mouse card 2   Cream, oval aperture 8.6 x 6.4cm (3⅜ x 2½in)

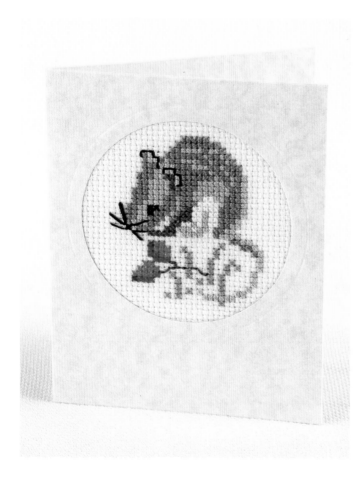

1

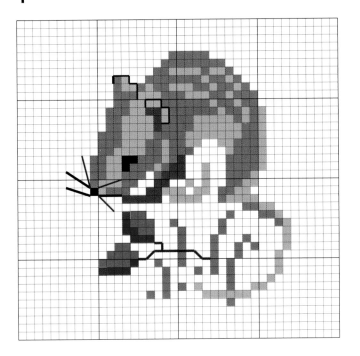

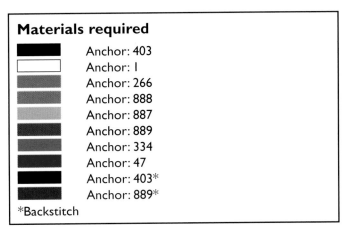

Design size	5.1 x 5.8cm (2 x 2⅓in)
Fabric	14-count Aida
Fabric count	14 holes per inch
Stitch	cross stitch
Stitch count	28 x 32
Stitch size	worked over every thread
Number of strands	2

Materials required

■	Anchor: 403
□	Anchor: 1
▨	Anchor: 266
▨	Anchor: 888
▨	Anchor: 887
▨	Anchor: 889
▨	Anchor: 334
▨	Anchor: 47
■	Anchor: 403*
▨	Anchor: 889*

*Backstitch

2

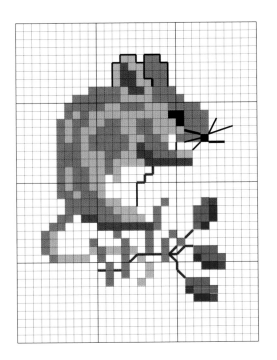

Design size	4.4 x 5.6cm (1⅞ x 2⅓in)
Fabric	14-count Aida
Fabric count	14 holes per inch
Stitch	cross stitch
Stitch count	24 x 31
Stitch size	worked on over every thread
Number of strands	2

DESIGNS FROM INDIA

INDIAN FLORAL BOOKMARK CARD

This bright card was adapted from a North Indian border design for textile printing. The orange and pink colours seemed, to me, to be typical of Indian saris. The border could easily be repeated to make it longer for a different purpose.

Card details:
Red bookmark card, aperture 13.5 x 3.1cm (5³⁄₁₀ x 1³⁄₁₀in)

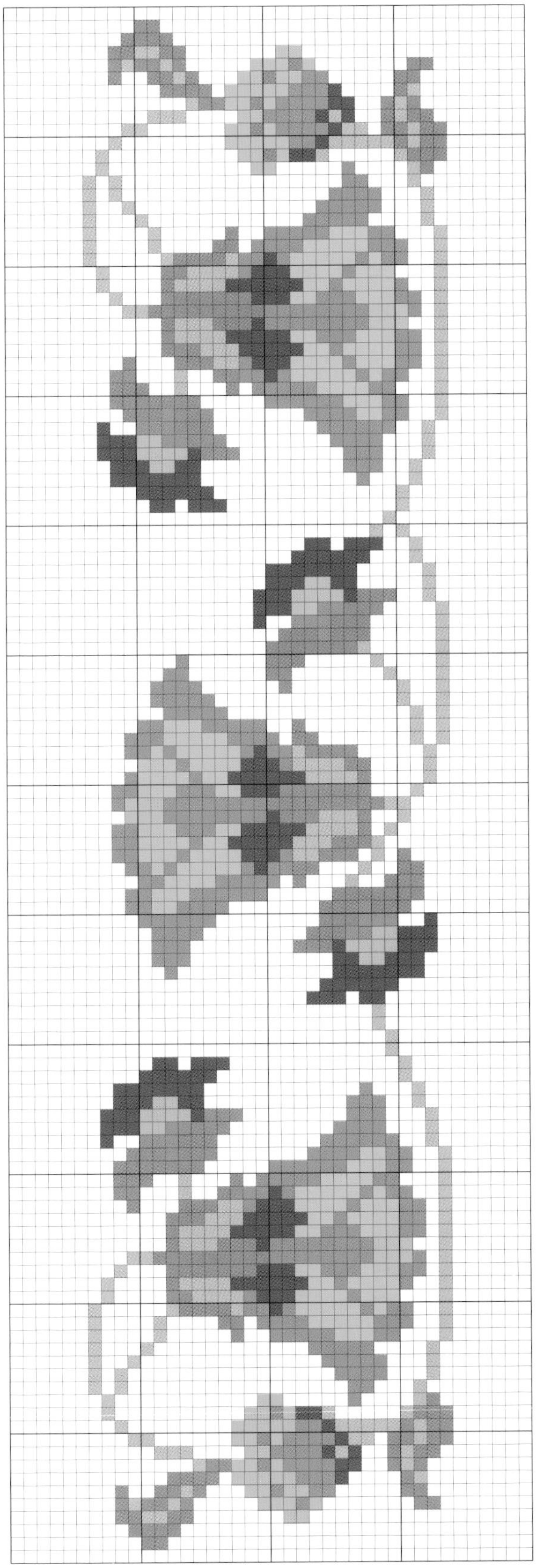

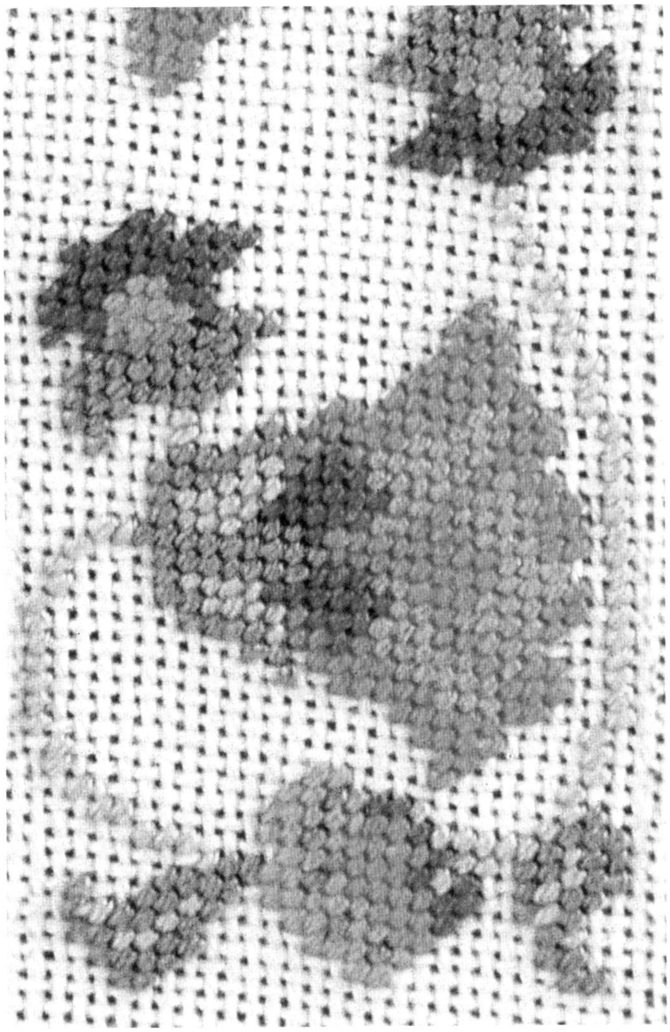

Design size	3.2 x 13.6cm ($1\frac{3}{10}$ x $5\frac{4}{10}$in)
Fabric count	22 holes per inch
Stitch	half-cross
Stitch count	28 x 118
Stitch size	worked over every thread
Number of strands	2

Materials required

- Anchor: 254
- Anchor: 255
- Anchor: 52
- Anchor: 38
- Anchor: 1014
- Anchor: 323

BLACKWORK CARDS AND GIFT TAGS

This simple block-printing leaf shape design from India cried out to be stitched using blackwork stitches. They are a way of filling the space within an outline with small repetitive patterns and are not difficult to do. If you are tentative about approaching blackwork, try one of the small gift tags first. I am sure you will soon want to tackle a card.

The easiest way to begin is to work the outline, using two strands of backstitch, and the stem, using two strands of cross stitch, then fill in the patterned centres using one strand, starting at the middle and working

outwards to the edges, and, finally, add the veins over the patterns. As the patterns form the decoration, colours tend to be limited to only one or two, and only one thread is used. I have worked the design using traditional black and also with a light variegated thread. As you can see, the results are quite different. I used 26-count fabric for the gift tags and worked over every thread. The pink one is half-cross stitch. The cards were worked on 28-count Jobelan over two threads.

Card details:

Blackwork leaf card   Dark green, oval aperture 15.2 x 10.8cm (6 x 4⅜in)
Variegated stitching card   Lilac Prisma felt effect, oval aperture 15.2 x 10.8cm (6 x 4⅜in)
Gift tags   White, circular aperture 4cm (1½in)

BLACKWORK LEAF CARD

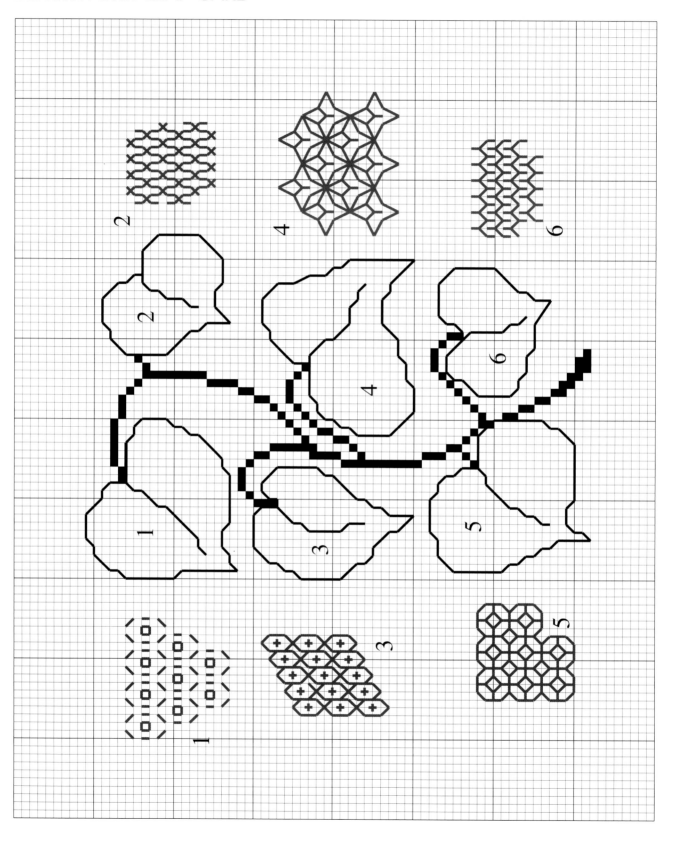

Design size	6.9 x 11.4cm (2⁷/₁₀ x 4½in)
Fabric	28-count Jobelan
Fabric count	14 holes per inch
Stitch	half-cross
Stitch count	42 x 63
Stitch size	worked over 2 threads

BLACKWORK GIFT TAGS

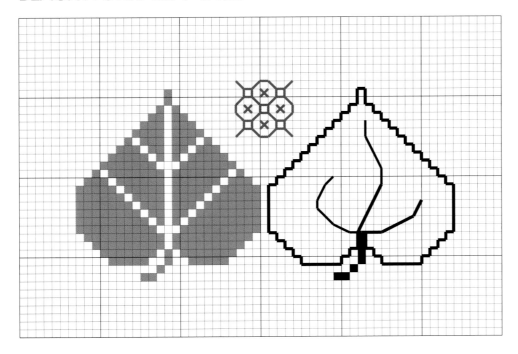

Design size	2.2 x 2.3cm (⁹/₁₀ x ⁹/₁₀in)
Fabric count	26 holes per inch
Stitch count	23 x 24
Stitch size	worked over every thread

MUGHAL ELEPHANT CARD

An elephant on a wall-hanging from Gujarat, western India, inspired this card. As you can probably tell, I thoroughly enjoyed decorating the stitching! The wall-hanging was so richly decorated that I could add as much gold thread, beads, sequins and shisha mirrors to the stitching as I liked to make a really lavish card.

When the chart had been worked, I fastened three dark red beads with half-crown covers along the bottom of the design and a gold shisha mirror on the cream stitching. I then hung two cream and two red beads with half-crown covers from another gold shisha mirror and fastened it to one corner of the card with a few stitches. To complete the card, I glued shisha mirrors at the remaining corners.

Card details:

Cream, rectangular aperture 13.9 x 9.5cm (5½ x 3⁷⁄₁₀in)

Design size	9.3 x 6.5cm (3⁷⁄₁₀ x 2⁹⁄₁₀in)
Fabric	28-count Jobelan
Fabric count	14 holes per inch
Stitch	cross stitch
Stitch count	51 x 36
Stitch size	worked over 2 threads
Number of strands	2

Materials required

	Anchor: 403
	Anchor: 398
	Anchor: 400/398
	Anchor: 46
	Anchor Perlé: 386*
	Anchor: 47
	Anchor Lamé: 303**
	Anchor: 400†
	Anchor: 46†
	8mm red sequin x 1
	Mill Hill Glass Seed beads: 02011 x 31

*Use whole thread
**Use 3 strands
†Backstitch

DESIGNS FROM EGYPT
EGYPTIAN MUMMY CARD

This design is made up of components from several wonderfully decorated coffins in the British Museum in London. These coffins were used to preserve the body so that it would be a place for the life force to rest. The internal organs were removed and the bodies were dried out using natural salt. They were then wrapped tightly in linen bandages before being placed in the coffins. A royal mummy was treated very elaborately: only the finest linen was used; the body was adorned with amulets and jewellery; and a gold mask was placed over the head and neck.

The small border design, which could be used on its own for another stitching project, is based on a pattern that occurs frequently in various forms throughout Egyptian designs.

Card details:

Egyptian mummy card – Dark green, rectangular aperture 13.3 x 8.9cm (5⁷⁄₁₀ x 3½in)

Egyptian head gift tag – Red gift tag, circular aperture 4cm (1½in)

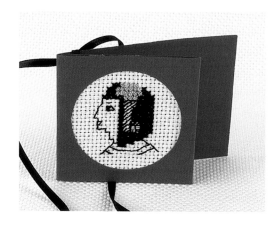

EGYPTIAN MUMMY CARD

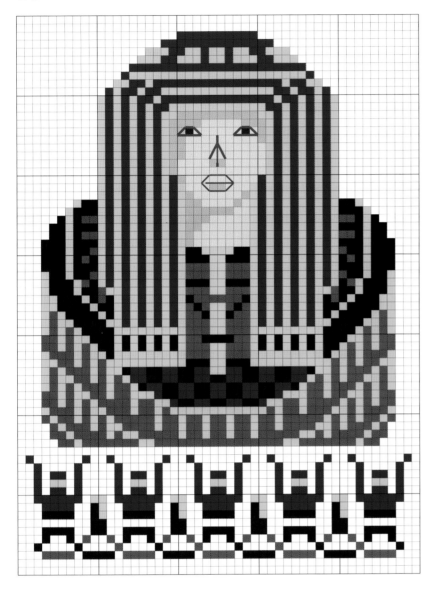

EGYPTIAN HEAD GIFT TAG

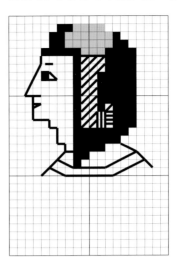

Design size	2.5 x 3cm (1 x 1³⁄₁₀in)
Fabric count	16 holes per inch
Stitch	cross stitch
Stitch count	16 x 19
Stitch size	worked over every thread
Number of strands	2

Materials required

■	Anchor: 403
▨	Anchor: Lamé 303*
■	Anchor: 403** †

*Use 3 strands
**Use 1 strand
†Backstitch

Design size	7.6 x 10.5cm (3 x 4¹⁄₁₀in)
Fabric count	16 holes per inch
Stitch	cross stitch
Stitch count	48 x 66
Stitch size	worked over every thread
Number of strands	2

Materials required

	Anchor: 236		Anchor: 217		Anchor: 236** †
	Anchor: 152		Anchor: 164		*Use 4 strands
	Anchor: 298/		Anchor: 926		** Use 1 strand
	Anchor Lamé: 303*		Anchor: 372		†Backstitch

HIEROGLYPHIC BOOKMARK CARD

The hieroglyphs on this bookmark card are not intended to give a message; they are simply a collection of the most frequently seen symbols in ancient Egyptian writing. Hieroglyphs are a form of symbolic writing: they represent sounds or parts of words. Some are pictographs, like an eye or flower, while others are ideographs; for example, an old man bent over a stick means 'old age', and a bird with a long, curved bill represents 'to find'. Hieroglyphs are usually read from the direction in which the figures or creatures are facing.

Card details:

Red bookmark card   aperture 3.5 x 3.1cm (1⅖ x 1⅕in)

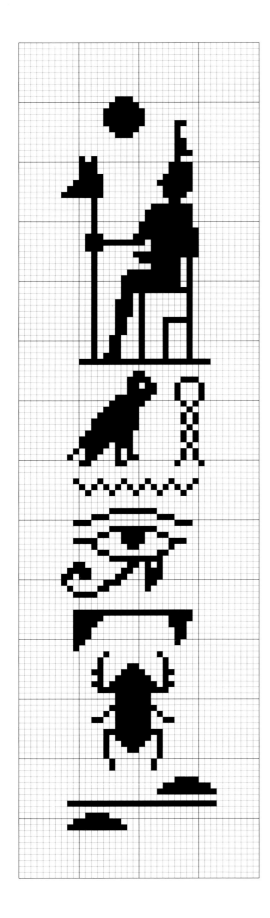

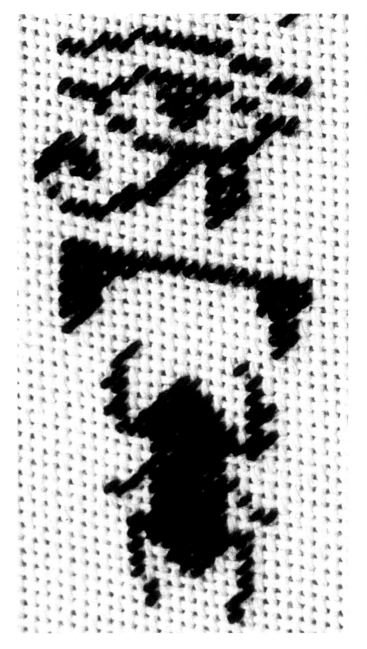

Design size	3 x 14.2cm (1³⁄₁₀ x 4⁵⁄₈in)
Fabric count	22 holes per inch
Stitch	half-cross
Stitch count	26 x 123
Stitch size	worked over every thread
Number of strands	2

Materials required

▬▬▬▬ Anchor: 403

DESIGNS FROM JAPAN

IMARI VASE CARD

This design, based on seventeenth century Japanese porcelain, is a card that ought to be framed and kept. It takes time to stitch but it is not difficult on this Easiweave fabric, and is beautiful when complete – well worth the effort for a very special occasion or a very special person! It would be an unusual card for a golden wedding, but it could have a golden 50 in the space at the bottom right – I am sure it would be much appreciated.

Card details:

Dark blue, circular aperture 12.6cm (5in)

Design size	11.1 x 10.6cm (4⁴⁄₁₀ x 4²⁄₁₀in)
Fabric count	19 holes per inch
Stitch	cross stitch
Stitch count	83 x 79
Stitch size	worked over every thread
Number of strands	2

Materials required

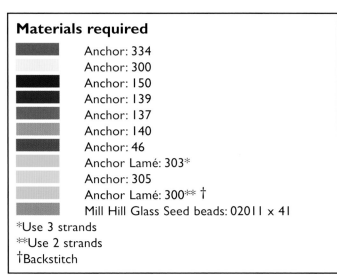

Anchor: 334
Anchor: 300
Anchor: 150
Anchor: 139
Anchor: 137
Anchor: 140
Anchor: 46
Anchor Lamé: 303*
Anchor: 305
Anchor Lamé: 300** †
Mill Hill Glass Seed beads: 02011 x 41

*Use 3 strands
**Use 2 strands
†Backstitch

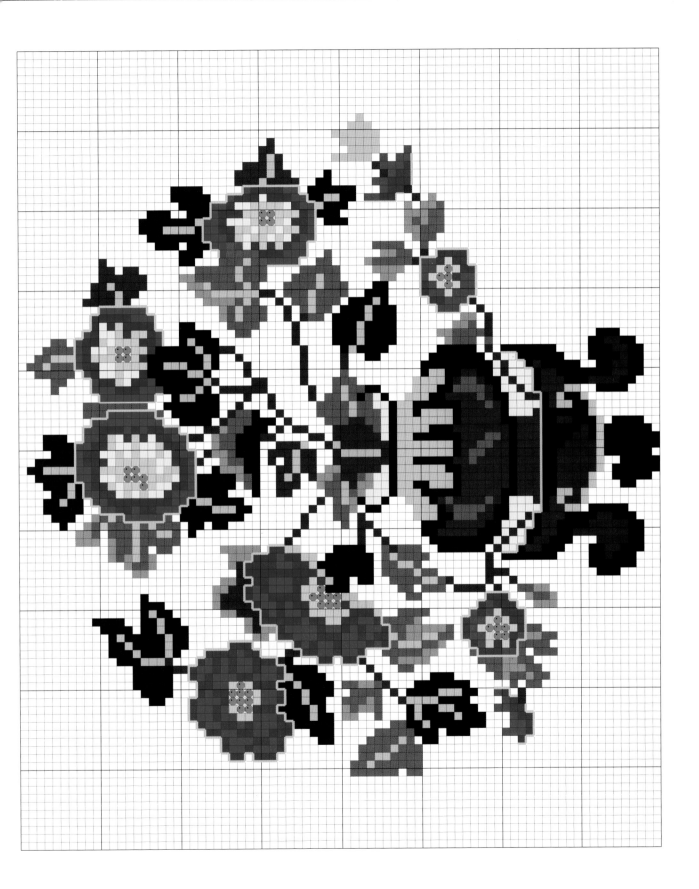

FISH CARD

Many wonderful designs in Japanese art represent carp, goldfish or Angel fish, and I think this card, stitched with a mixture of metallic and matt thread, has retained the lively character of many of these fish designs. I have used a hand-dyed imitation silk thread, available by mail order from De Haviland. This mixed green and blue thread has been used in several designs in the book, but I only used one hank to stitch all of these designs, including the large sampler, and I have a surplus!

If working on black is a new experience for you, make sure you have a good light. If you put a light-coloured cloth on your knee the black strands will be clearly defined and you should not have a problem. The need for good light is also the reason I like to stitch any work on black fabric outside on a sunny day. The silver line on this bright white card from Framecraft Miniatures really sets off the design.

Card details:
White, oval aperture
13.9 x 9.5cm (5½ x 3⁷⁄₁₀in)

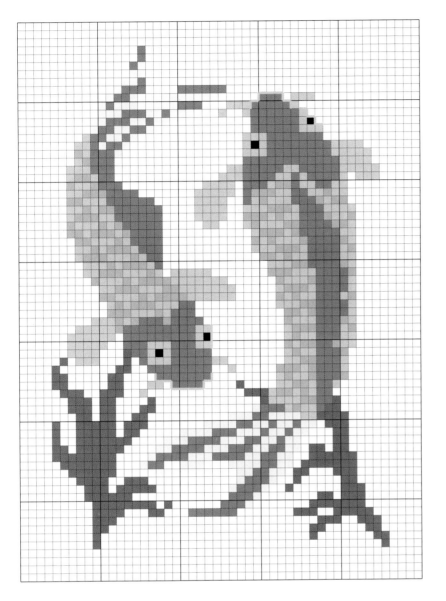

Design size	7.6 x 11.4cm (3 x 4½in)
Fabric	black 28-count Jobelan
Fabric count	14 holes per inch
Stitch	cross stitch
Stitch count	42 x 63
Stitch size	worked over 2 threads
Number of strands	2

Materials required

■	Anchor: 403
	Anchor: 1037
	De Haviland: blue/green**
	Kreinik Blending Filament: 014
	Coats Ophir silver: 301
	Kreinik Blending filament: 015HL
	Coats Ophir silver: 301*

*Backstitch
**Use 2 strands

DESIGNS FROM NORTH AMERICA
DREAM-CATCHER CARD

According to American legend, dream-catchers look after us while we are asleep. Good dreams enter through the centre hole and float down to the sleeper, while bad dreams are caught in the web. It holds them until the morning light when they evaporate in the sun's rays. Any that remain are turned into dew, which travels down the feathers and back into the earth.

I used a collection of odd beads and feathers to finish off the rustic card. The feather shafts are glued through the hole in the bead.

Card details:
Light cream, circular aperture 9.5cm (3⅞in)

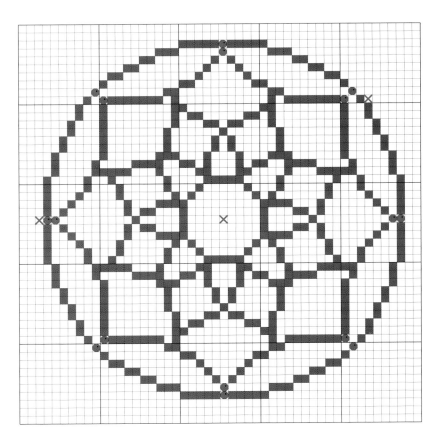

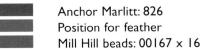

Materials required

	Anchor Marlitt: 826
	Position for feather
	Mill Hill beads: 00167 x 16

Design size	6.5 x 6.4cm (2½ x 2½in)
Fabric	rustic 18-count fabric
Fabric count	18 holes per inch
Stitch	cross stitch
Stitch count	46 x 45
Stitch size	worked over every thread
Number of strands	2

BEADED BOOKMARK CARD AND GIFT TAG

This card and gift tag feature a compilation of patterns from North American beadwork. These brightly-coloured patterns enliven pouches, knife covers, belts, headbands and many other articles of clothing. The beadwork patterns are varied: some feature geometric, floral or animal designs; others are representational, such as a jagged line, which stands for lightning, and a cross, which signifies the four winds.

I have stitched the cards in half-cross stitch on 22- and 28-count fabric and used Anchor Marlitt thread, as this has a sheen. I added strings of Mill Hill beads (03038, 03043, 00423, 00167) for a finishing touch. The cards could also be stitched using Anchor stranded cotton (substitute 256, 846, 326 and 323 for 1030, 826 1045 and 850).

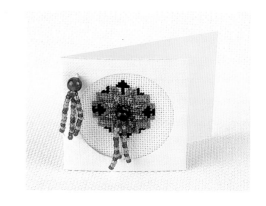

Card details:

Gift tag	Cream, circular aperture 4cm (1½in)
Bookmark cards	Cream, aperture 13.5 x 3.1cm (5⁵⁄₁₀ x 1⁷⁄₁₀in)

BEADED GIFT TAG

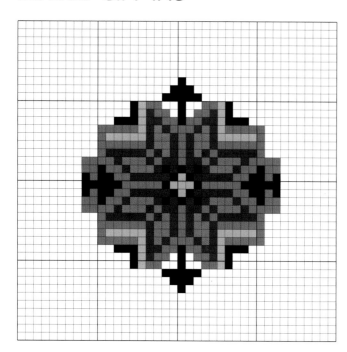

Design size	2.9 x 3.1cm (1¹⁄₁₀ x 1³⁄₁₀in)
Fabric count	22 holes per inch
Stitch	half-cross
Stitch count	25 x 27
Stitch size	worked over every thread
Number of strands	2

Materials required

■	Anchor: 403
	Anchor Marlitt: 1030
	Anchor Marlitt: 826
	Anchor Marlitt: 1045
	Anchor Marlitt: 850

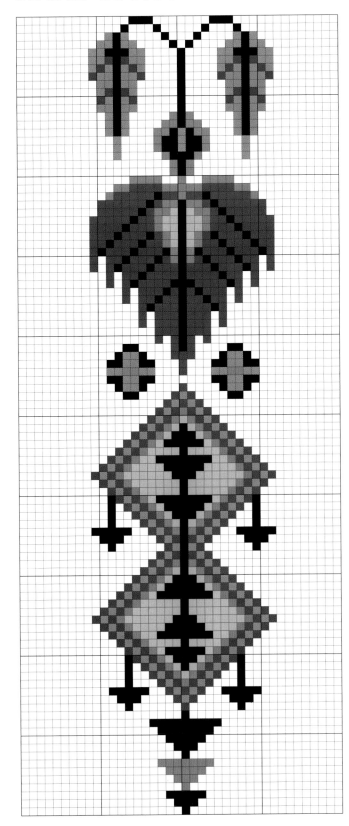

BEADED BOOKMARK CARD

Design size	2.1 x 9.1cm (⅚ x 3⅗in)
Fabric count	28 holes per inch
Stitch	half-cross
Stitch count	23 x 100
Stitch size	worked over every thread
Number of strands	2

Materials required

■	Anchor: 403
	Anchor Marlitt: 1030
	Anchor Marlitt: 826
	Anchor Marlitt: 1045
	Anchor Marlitt: 850

NORTH AMERICAN MOTIF BOOKMARK CARD

This design features a border from moccasins, plus three North American motifs: an eagle, buffalo and deer. Set in this green card it becomes a lively bookmark. If you wanted to personalize this design, an initial could be stitched above or below the design and the completed stitching could be centred in the card.

Card details:

Green bookmark card, aperture 4cm (1½in)

Design size	2.3 x 10.1cm (⅞ x 4in)
Fabric count	28 holes per inch
Stitch	half-cross
Stitch count	25 x 111
Stitch size	worked over every thread
Number of strands	2

Materials required

■	Anchor: 403
▨	Anchor Marlitt: 1030
▨	Anchor Marlitt: 826
▨	Anchor Marlitt: 1045
▨	Anchor Marlitt: 850
▨	Anchor: 403*

*Full-cross stitch

GALLERY OF GENERAL CARD DESIGNS

ABSTRACT FLORAL CARDS

Both these designs are taken from a chintz design, dated 1877. They look particularly vibrant stitched in these colours on black fabric, and the beads shine beautifully in the light. The bright white cards from Framecraft Miniatures frame them perfectly.

Card details:
White, rectangular aperture 13.9 x 9.5cm (5½ x 3⅞in)

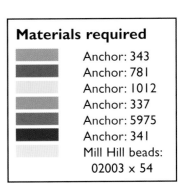

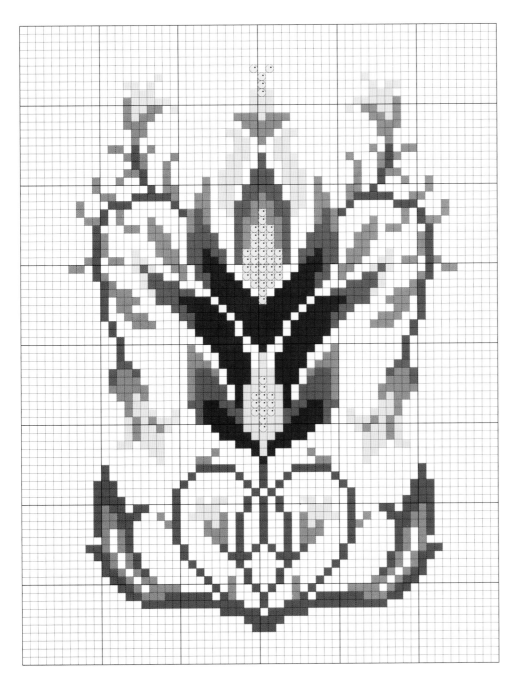

Materials required

	Anchor: 343
	Anchor: 781
	Anchor: 1012
	Anchor: 337
	Anchor: 5975
	Anchor: 341
	Mill Hill beads: 02003 x 54

Design size	8.9 x 12.9cm (3½ x 5in)
Fabric	black 28-count Jobelan
Fabric count	14 holes per inch
Stitch	cross stitch
Stitch count	49 x 71
Stitch size	worked over 2 threads
Number of strands	2

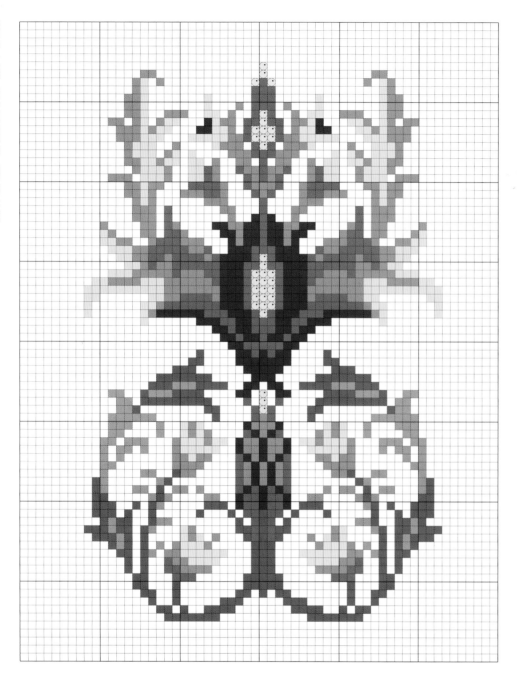

Design size	8.2 x 12.7cm (3³/₁₀ x 5in)
Fabric	black 28-count Jobelan
Fabric count	14 holes per inch
Stitch	cross stitch
Stitch count	45 x 70
Stitch size	worked over 2 threads
Number of strands	2

Materials required

Mill Hill beads: 02003 x 34
*Refer to card 1 for threads required

CLOWN CARD

This would be a lively card for a child's birthday, and the basic stitched design can be adapted if you wish: the initial on the ball could be changed to a number, and a name could be fitted to the left side. I added a green pom-pom from a Christmas pack to the top of the hat, but a large sequin could replace this. I made two small bows from 0.5cm (¼in) hair-ribbon and fastened them onto the shoes, then stitched a small gold sequin to the hat, and finished the card off by gluing shisha mirrors at each corner which reflect the light. Altogether a jolly card to send!

Card details:
Cobalt Prisma felt-effect, oval aperture 17.8 x 12.7cm (7 x 5in)

CLOWN CARD

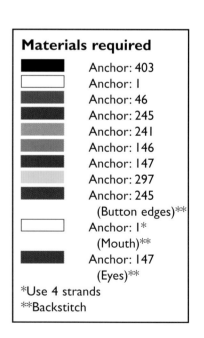

Materials required

■	Anchor: 403
□	Anchor: 1
▨	Anchor: 46
▨	Anchor: 245
▨	Anchor: 241
▨	Anchor: 146
▨	Anchor: 147
▨	Anchor: 297
▨	Anchor: 245 (Button edges)**
□	Anchor: 1* (Mouth)**
■	Anchor: 147 (Eyes)**

*Use 4 strands
**Backstitch

Design size	8.2 x 13.4cm (3³⁄₁₀ x 5³⁄₁₀in)
Fabric	28-count Jobelan
Fabric count	14 holes per inch
Stitch	cross stitch
Stitch count	45 x 74
Stitch size	worked over 2 threads
Number of strands	2

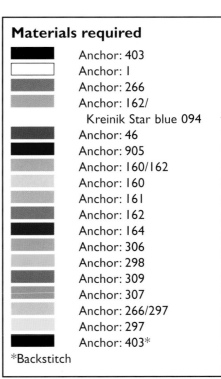

KINGFISHER CARD

To me, kingfishers are special. They are so brilliantly coloured and easily recognizable, yet so rarely seen except by a few lucky people. This card takes longer to stitch than some of the others, but the finished result, with touches of metallic thread, is well worth the effort and I am sure would be appreciated by anyone, whether they are an ornithologist or not!

Card details:

White, oval aperture 13.9 x 9.5cm (5½ x 3⁷⁄₁₀in)

Materials required

■	Anchor: 403
□	Anchor: 1
▨	Anchor: 266
▨	Anchor: 162/
	Kreinik Star blue 094
▨	Anchor: 46
■	Anchor: 905
▨	Anchor: 160/162
▨	Anchor: 160
▨	Anchor: 161
▨	Anchor: 162
▨	Anchor: 164
▨	Anchor: 306
▨	Anchor: 298
▨	Anchor: 309
▨	Anchor: 307
▨	Anchor: 266/297
▨	Anchor: 297
■	Anchor: 403*

*Backstitch

119

KINGFISHER CARD

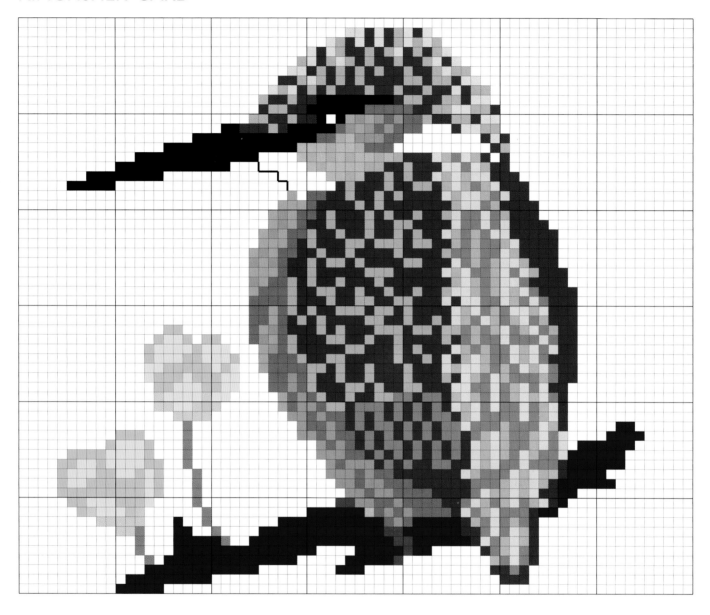

Design size	9.7 x 9.4cm (3⁸⁄₁₀ x 3⁷⁄₁₀in)
Fabric count	16 holes per inch
Stitch	cross stitch
Stitch count	61 x 59
Stitch size	worked over every thread
Number of strands	2

COUNTRY COTTAGE CARD

This is a small, useful design that would make a nice birthday card or 'new home' card. There is room at the bottom for a message. Add a few ready-made flower motifs at the bottom right-hand corner of the card to finish it off.

Card details:
White Lorenzo parchment effect, oval aperture 10.2 x 7.9cm (4 x 3¹⁄₁₀in)

COUNTRY COTTAGE CARD

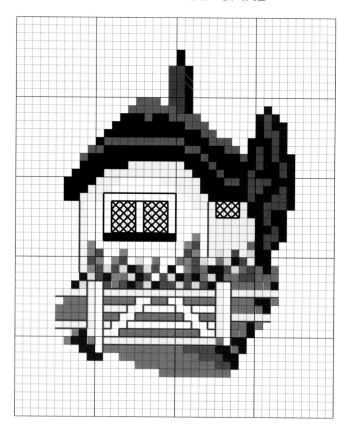

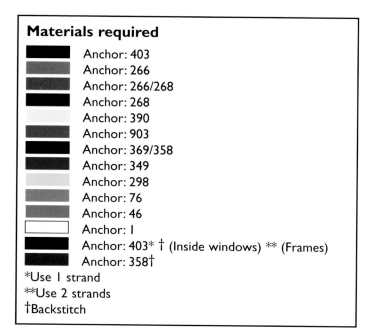

Materials required

■	Anchor: 403
■	Anchor: 266
■	Anchor: 266/268
■	Anchor: 268
░	Anchor: 390
■	Anchor: 903
■	Anchor: 369/358
■	Anchor: 349
░	Anchor: 298
■	Anchor: 76
■	Anchor: 46
□	Anchor: 1
■	Anchor: 403* † (Inside windows) ** (Frames)
■	Anchor: 358†

*Use 1 strand
**Use 2 strands
†Backstitch

Design size	5.4 x 7.4cm (2¹⁄₁₀ x 2⁹⁄₁₀in)
Fabric	14-count Aida
Fabric count	14 holes per inch
Stitch	cross stitch
Stitch count	30 x 41
Stitch size	worked over every thread
Number of strands	2

TUDOR HOUSE CARD

This is another card that would be suitable for celebrating a new home. Again, by positioning the design further up or down in the aperture, there could be room for a message.

Card details:
Dark green, oval aperture 13.3 x 8.9cm (5⅕ x 3½in)

TUDOR HOUSE CARD

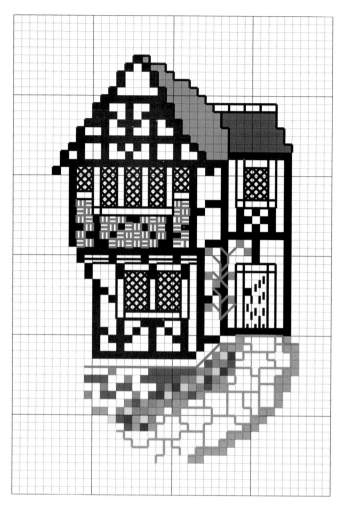

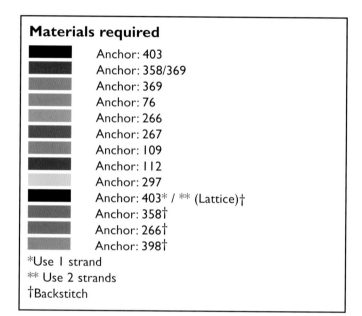

Materials required

■	Anchor: 403
■	Anchor: 358/369
■	Anchor: 369
■	Anchor: 76
■	Anchor: 266
■	Anchor: 267
■	Anchor: 109
■	Anchor: 112
▨	Anchor: 297
■	Anchor: 403* / ** (Lattice)†
■	Anchor: 358†
■	Anchor: 266†
■	Anchor: 398†

*Use 1 strand
** Use 2 strands
†Backstitch

Design size	5.6 x 9.3cm (2³⁄₁₀ x 3⁵⁄₁₀in)
Fabric	28-count Jobelan
Fabric count	14 holes per inch
Stitch	cross stitch
Stitch count	31 x 51
Stitch size	worked over 2 threads
Number of strands	2

GIRAFFE BOOKMARK CARD

Giraffes are among my favourite creatures, so I had to include this design. Obviously, the initial could be changed, and the daisy chain is only there for a bit of fun!

Card details:

Green bookmark card, aperture
13.5 x 3.1cm (5³⁄₁₀ x 1²⁄₁₀in)

Design size	2.5 x 12.7cm (1 x 5in)
Fabric count	16 holes per inch
Stitch	cross stitch
Stitch count	16 x 80
Stitch size	worked over every thread
Number of strands	2

Materials required

⬛	Anchor: 403
⬛	Anchor: 246
▦	Anchor: 371/369
▨	Anchor: 358/369
▦	Anchor: 905
▨	Anchor: 903/371
▨	Anchor: 390/899
▧	Anchor: 390
⬛	Anchor: 403* **

*Use 1 strand
**Backstitch

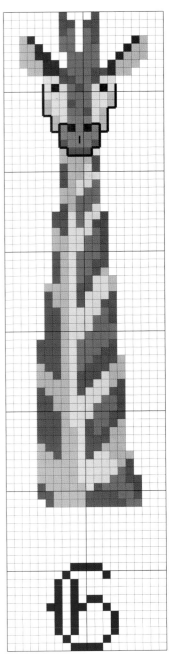

ART NOUVEAU FLORAL CARDS AND GIFT TAG

Art Nouveau designs lend themselves to stitching because they have such clean lines of colour. I have designed three cards and a gift tag, each one being quick to stitch, yet effective when complete. I added a finishing touch to the blue and green card and tag by putting together a length of green and blue 0.5cm (¼in) width ribbon and tying a small bow.

Card details:

Carnation bookmark card	Cream bookmark card, aperture 13.5 x 3.1cm (5³⁄₁₀ x 1²⁄₁₀in)
Pink and green card	Cream, oval aperture 8.6 x 6.4cm (3⁴⁄₁₀ x 2½in)
Blue and green card	Bright white, square aperture 5.4cm (2in)
Blue and green gift tag	White, circular aperture 4cm (1½in)

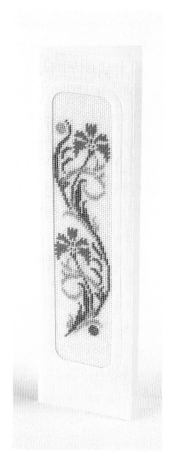

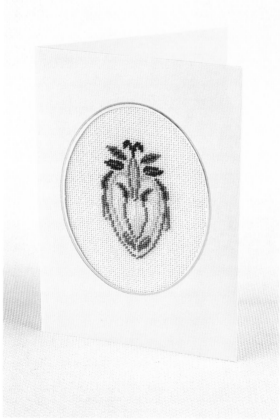

CARNATION BOOKMARK CARD

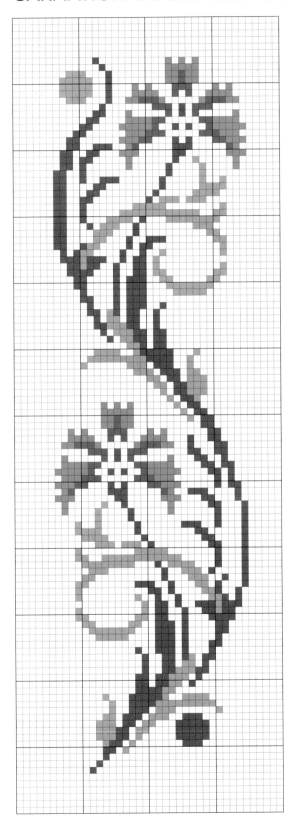

Design size	3.3 x 12.5cm (1⅒ x 4⅘in)
Fabric count	22 holes per inch
Stitch	half-cross
Stitch count	29 x 108
Stitch size	worked over every thread
Number of strands	2

Materials required

	Anchor: 842
	Anchor: 843
	Anchor: 10
	Anchor: 35

BLUE AND GREEN GIFT TAG

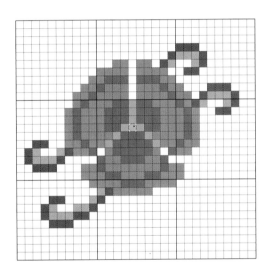

Design size	3.1 x 2.7cm (1⅒ x 1in)
Fabric count	22 holes per inch
Stitch	half-cross
Stitch count	27 x 23
Stitch size	worked over every thread
Number of strands	2

Materials required

	Mill Hill beads: 00168 x 1

*Refer to the blue and green card for threads required

PINK AND GREEN CARD

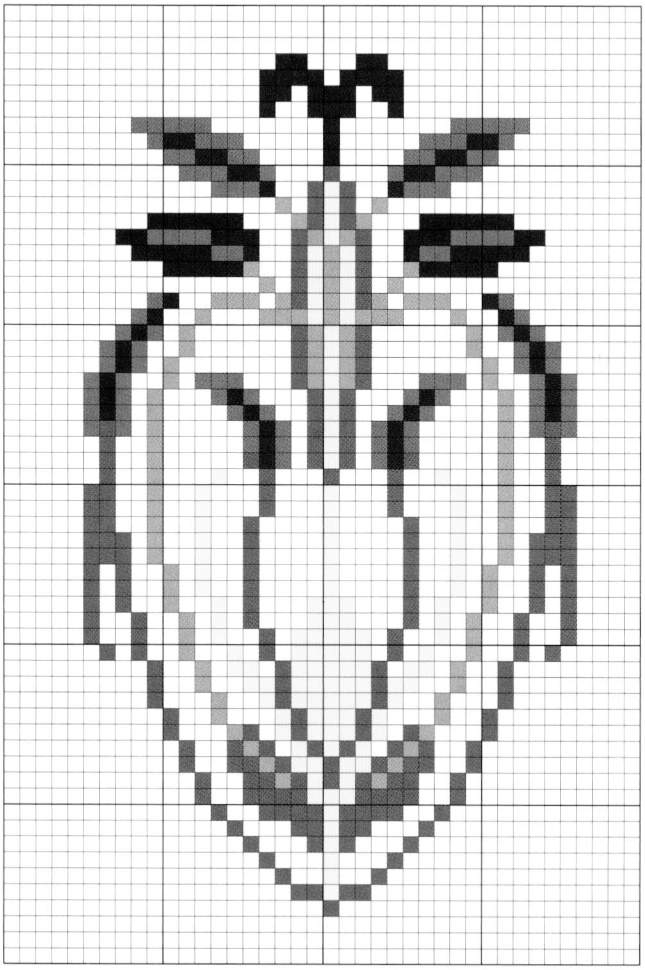

Design size	3.6 x 6.2cm ($1\frac{4}{10}$ x $2\frac{1}{2}$in)
Fabric count	22 holes per inch
Stitch	half-cross
Stitch count	31 x 54
Stitch size	worked over every thread
Number of strands	2

Materials required

Anchor: 386
Anchor: 897
Anchor: 205
Anchor: 1027
Anchor: 206

BLUE AND GREEN CARD

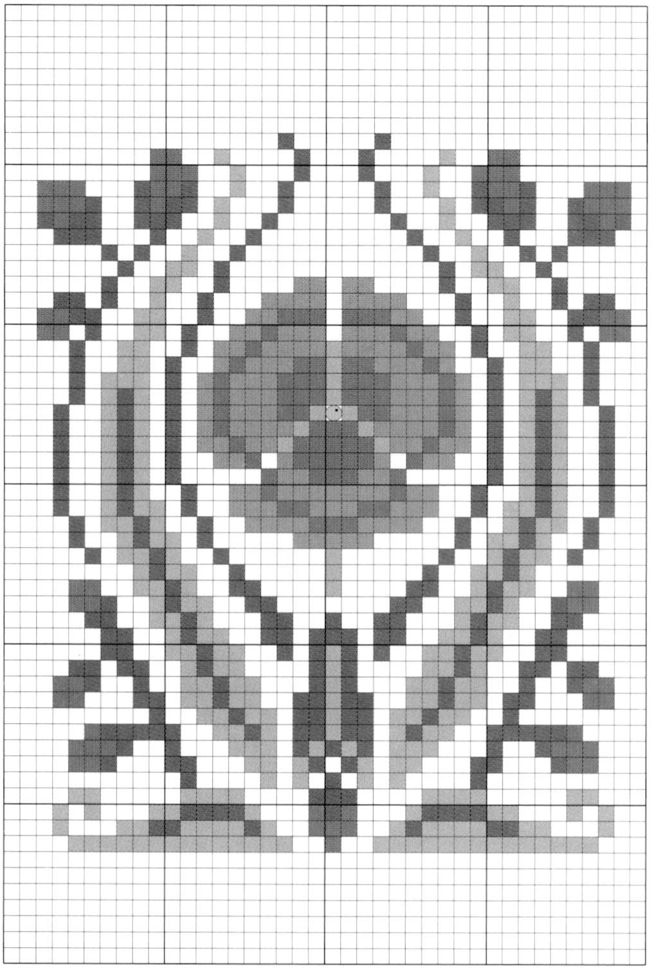

Design size	3.6 x 4.4cm ($1\frac{4}{10}$ x $1\frac{7}{10}$in)
Fabric count	26 holes per inch
Stitch	half-cross
Stitch count	37 x 45
Stitch size	worked over every thread
Number of strands	2

Materials required

Anchor: 118
Anchor: 117
Anchor: 206
Anchor: 216
Mill Hill beads: 00168 x 4

WEDGWOOD CARD

The inspiration for this card came from an old urn made by Wedgwood. It is stitched in cream Perlé cotton, which, when worked on this airforce blue Jobelan, gives just the right appearance. The design is worked in cross stitch, half-cross stitch and has a cluster of French knots, so it is quite textured. If you are not particularly confident about working the knots, try one or two on a spare piece of fabric, following the instructions on page 5. But don't worry about getting them all perfect because, as there are several of them filling an area, one wrong knot can easily be lost!

Card details:
Cream, oval aperture 13.9 x 9.5cm (5½ x 3⅞in)

WEDGWOOD CARD

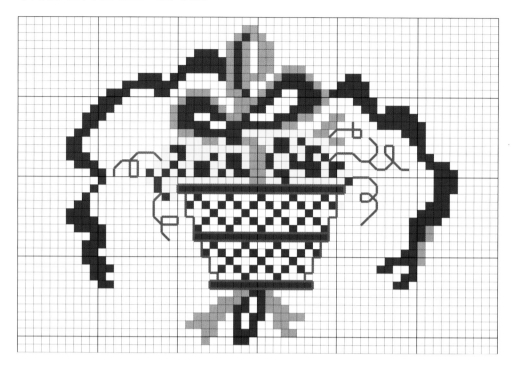

Design size	8.9 x 7.3cm (3½ x 2⅞in)
Fabric	blue 28-count Jobelan
Fabric count	14 holes per inch
Stitch	cross stitch
Stitch count	49 x 40
Stitch size	worked over 2 threads
Number of strands	2

Materials required

	Anchor Perlé: 386*
	Anchor Perlé: 386**
	Anchor Perlé: 386
	Anchor Perlé: 386†

*Half-cross
**French knots
†Backstitch

IZNIK POTTERY CARD

The unusual shape of this card provides added interest to the design. It is thought that about four thousand bowls and plates survive from the Iznik pottery in Turkey, and this design is based on plates from the 'Damascus' group, which was produced between 1520 and 1555. The plates were mistakenly thought to have come from Damascus, hence their name.

Card details:
Bright white angled oval, aperture 9.8 x 6.1cm (3⁹⁄₁₀ x 2⁶⁄₁₀in)

IZNIK POTTERY CARD

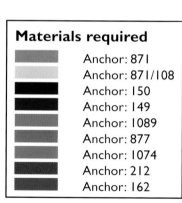

Materials required

	Anchor: 871
	Anchor: 871/108
	Anchor: 150
	Anchor: 149
	Anchor: 1089
	Anchor: 877
	Anchor: 1074
	Anchor: 212
	Anchor: 162

Design size	6.1 x 7.5cm (2⁹⁄₁₀ x 3in)
Fabric count	22 holes per inch
Stitch	half-cross
Stitch count	53 x 65
Stitch size	worked over every thread
Number of strands	2

ROSE HARDANGER CARD

I based this design on hardanger patterns. It is a pretty card and the addition of the flowers and beads provides an extra special touch. The rosebud, when stitched in half-cross stitch on 22-count fabric, fits into a 4cm (1½in) aperture for a gift tag.

Card details:

White, rectangular aperture 13.9 x 9.5cm (5½ x 3⅞in)

Materials required

▬	Anchor: 216
▬	Anchor: 879
▬	Anchor: 214
▬	Anchor: 969
▬	Anchor: 970
▬	Anchor: 968
	Mill Hill beads: 00123 x16

Design size	8.9 x 13.2cm (3½ x 5⅖in)
Fabric count	16 holes per inch
Stitch	cross stitch
Stitch count	56 x 83
Stitch size	worked over every thread
Number of strands	2

ROSE HARDANGER CARD

TULIP HARDANGER CARD

This design was also derived from hardanger patterns but is brighter and more dramatic than the rose card. Again, the addition of beads, and this time also a bow, makes it quite distinctive.

Card details:
White, rectangular aperture 13.9 x 9.5cm (5½ x 3⅞in)

Materials required

	Anchor: 122
	Anchor: 127
	Anchor: 101
	Anchor: 137
	Anchor: 205
	Mill Hill beads: 03026 x 12
	Mill Hill beads: 00123 x 10

Design size	9.4 x 13cm (3⅞ x 5⅛in)
Fabric count	16 holes per inch
Stitch	cross stitch
Stitch count	59 x 82
Stitch size	worked over every thread
Number of strands	2

TULIP HARDANGER CARD

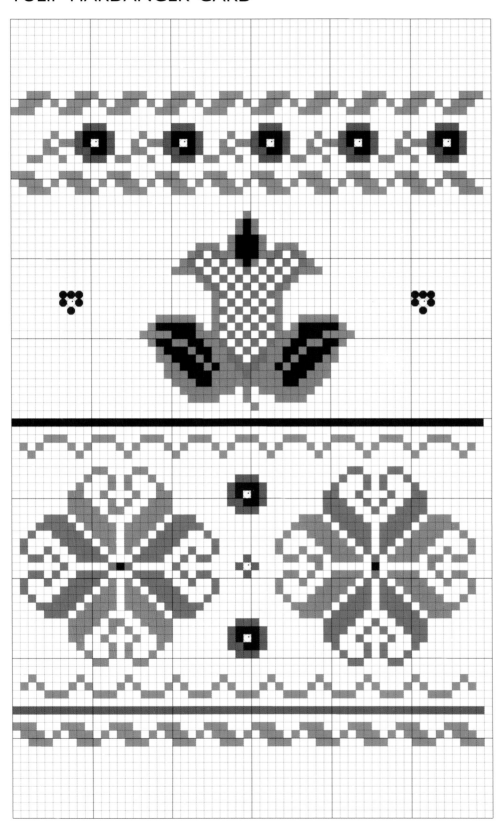

SPANIEL CARD

This is a simple yet effective and lifelike design that is obviously particularly suitable for sending to a dog-lover. It would also make a lovely small picture.

Card details:
Cream, oval aperture 13.9 x 9.5cm (5½ x 3⁷⁄₁₀in)

SPANIEL CARD

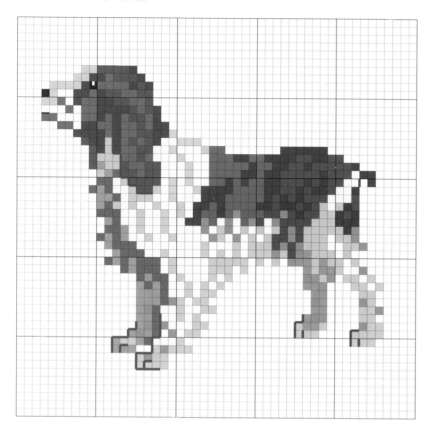

Design size	7.8 x 6.9cm (3 x 2¾in)
Fabric	28-count Jobelan
Fabric count	14 holes per inch
Stitch	cross stitch
Stitch count	43 x 38
Stitch size	worked over 2 threads
Number of strands	2

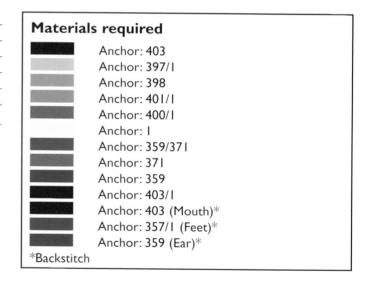

Materials required

Anchor: 403
Anchor: 397/1
Anchor: 398
Anchor: 401/1
Anchor: 400/1
Anchor: 1
Anchor: 359/371
Anchor: 371
Anchor: 359
Anchor: 403/1
Anchor: 403 (Mouth)*
Anchor: 357/1 (Feet)*
Anchor: 359 (Ear)*

*Backstitch

GOLD CROWN CARD

The inspiration for this dainty card came from a design I saw in a book on ornamental interiors. It incorporates an Islamic lozenge shape with lilies, which symbolize purity, encircled by a crown.

Card details:
Cream, oval aperture 8.6 x 6.4cm (3³⁄₁₀ x 2½in)

GOLD CROWN CARD

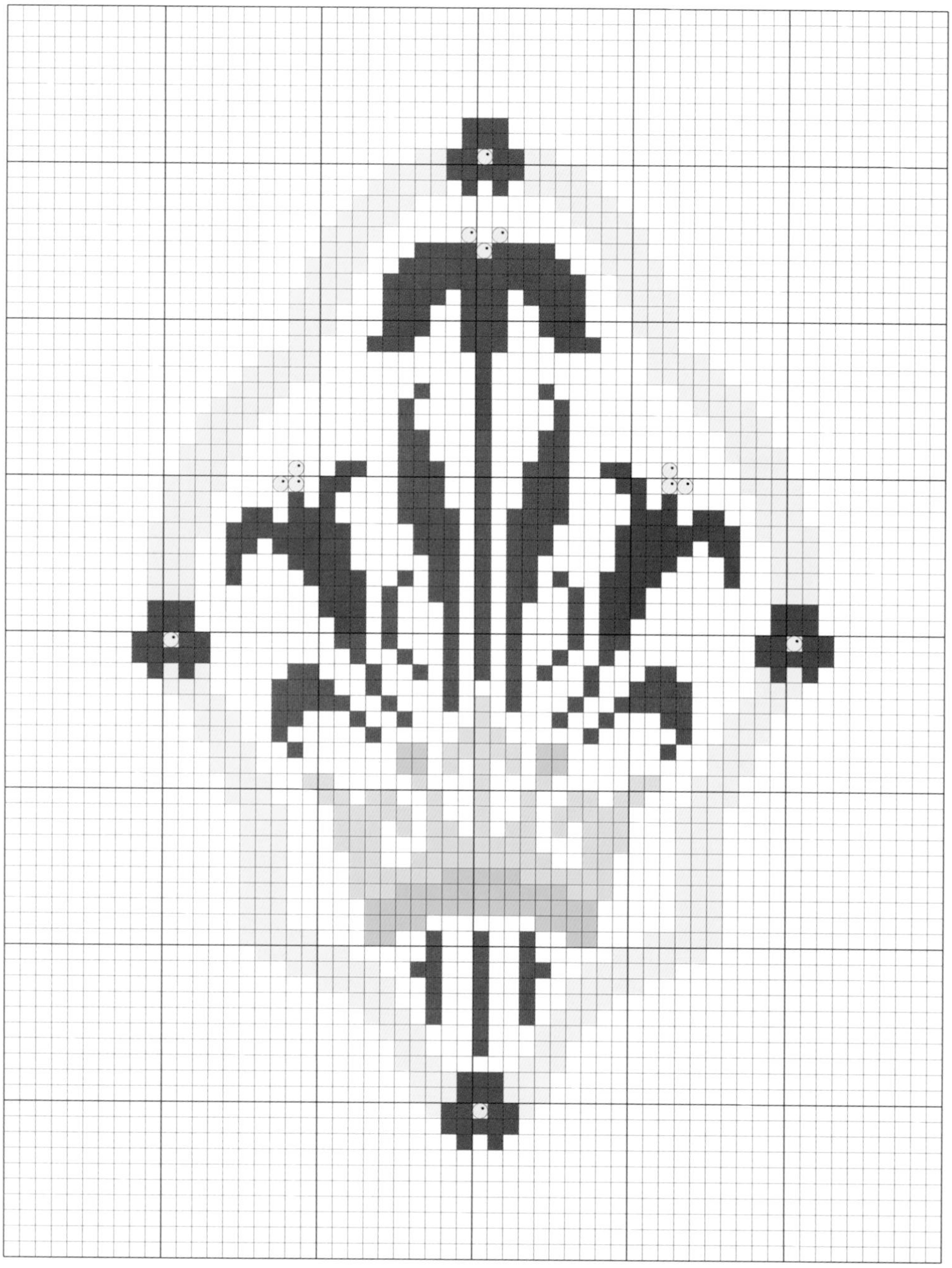

Design size	5.2 x 7.6cm (2 x 3in)
Fabric count	22 holes per inch
Stitch	half-cross
Stitch count	45 x 66
Stitch size	worked over every thread
Number of strands	2

Materials required

- Anchor: 227
- Anchor: 298
- Anchor Lamé: 300*
- Anchor Lamé: 303*
- Anchor: 94 or De Haviland purple
- Mill Hill Glass Seed Beads: 40557 x 16

*Use 3 strands

TOADSTOOLS CARD

Fly Agaric toadstools, the variety that appear in fairy story illustrations, are stitched here to make an unusual card.

Card details:

Natural Lorenzo parchment effect, oval aperture 7.6 x 5cm (3 x 2in)

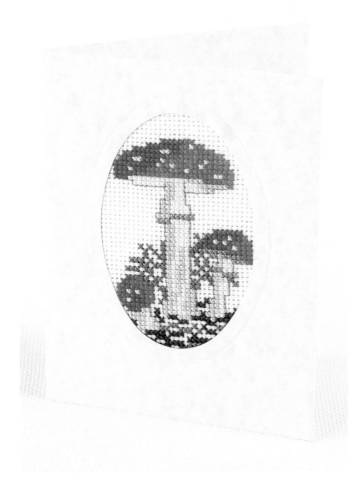

Materials required

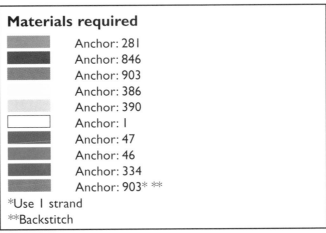

	Anchor: 281
	Anchor: 846
	Anchor: 903
	Anchor: 386
	Anchor: 390
	Anchor: 1
	Anchor: 47
	Anchor: 46
	Anchor: 334
	Anchor: 903* **

*Use 1 strand
**Backstitch

Design size	4.6 x 7.3cm (1⁹⁄₁₀ x 2⁹⁄₁₀in)
Fabric count	16 holes per inch
Stitch	cross stitch
Stitch count	29 x 46
Stitch size	worked over every thread
Number of strands	2

ALPHABET SAMPLER PROJECTS

I thought it necessary to provide a selection of alphabets so that any of the cards could be personalized with an appropriate message. The alphabets are adapted from both old and modern samplers to give a selection of styles and sizes. Instead of just supplying charts, I decided it would be more enjoyable to make the alphabets into samplers, which then enables larger, more challenging projects to be stitched.

ALPHABET SAMPLER

The alphabets in this sampler are in cross stitch and backstitch, but some other easy counted-thread stitches have been used to create texture. The instructions for these are given at the beginning of the book on pages 4–5. For Rhodes Stitch and Eyelet Stitch I have given the outline size of the stitch and the direction of the first stitch on the chart.

I have only used two different threads here, but the finished result is quite stunning. The cream thread is Perlé Cotton 8, number 386, and two bobbins are needed. For the darker thread I have used a variegated thread. This could be changed to your personal choice. I used a hand-dyed imitation silk thread, available by mail order from De Haviland and used two strands. One skein will stitch all of the items where it is needed in the book. Any stranded cotton can replace this but two skeins will be needed.

The sampler is stitched on 28-count Jobelan worked over two threads, so any 14-count fabric could be substituted. You will need a piece of fabric that is approximately 48 x 38cm (19 x 15in).

Start stitching in the centre and work out to the Rhodes border, then work the border as a frame in which to place the other stitching.

When the stitching is complete, press on the wrong side onto a padded surface using a damp cloth (I use a folded towel as padding), then stretch and frame as you wish.

Design size	28.8 x 33.2cm (11⅜ x 13in)
Fabric	28-count Jobelan
Fabric count	14 holes per inch
Stitch	counted thread
Stitch count	159 x 183
Stitch size	worked over 2 threads
Number of strands	2

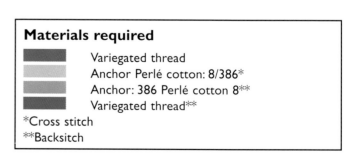

Materials required

■	Variegated thread
▨	Anchor Perlé cotton: 8/386*
▨	Anchor: 386 Perlé cotton 8**
■	Variegated thread**

*Cross stitch
**Backsitch

ABCDEFGHIJKLM
NOPQRSTUVWXYZ
ABCDEFGHIJKLMNOPQRSTUVWXYZ
abcdefghijklmnopqrstuvwxyz
1234567890

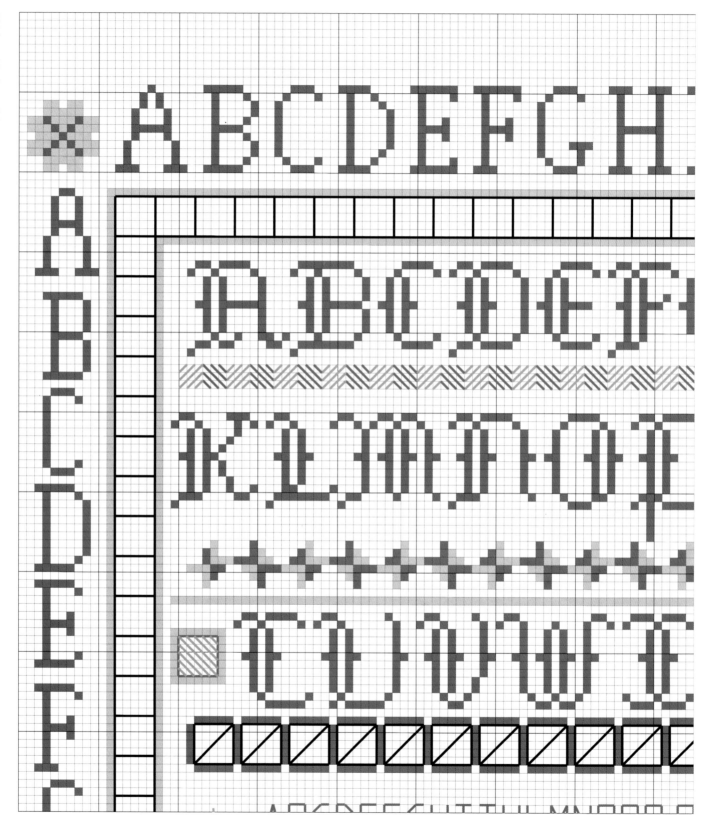

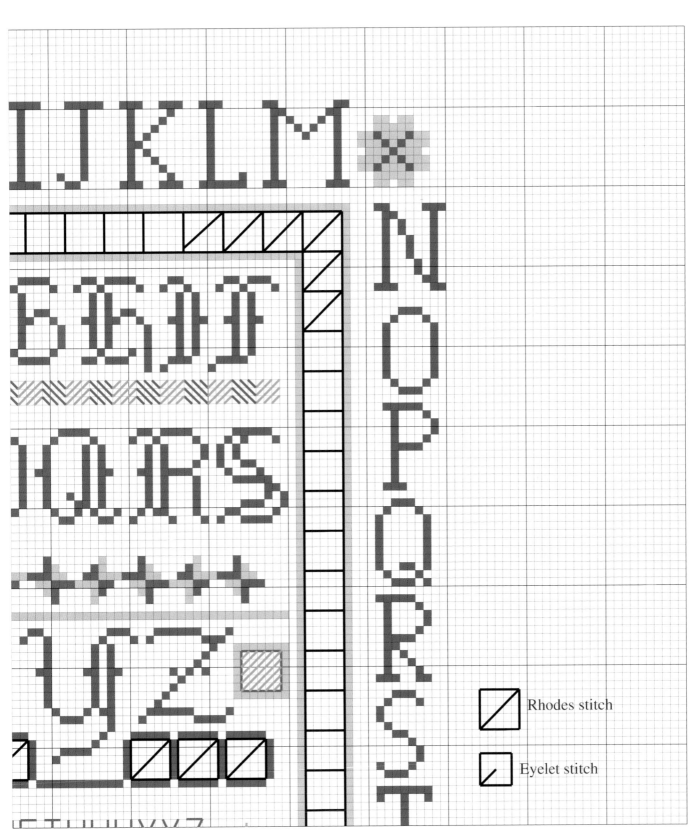

Rhodes stitch

Eyelet stitch

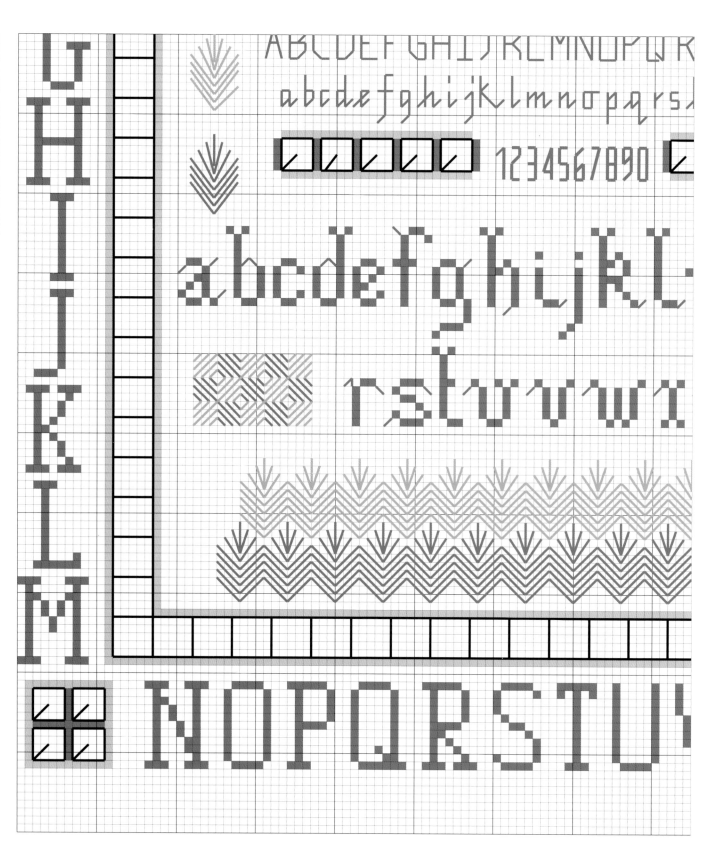

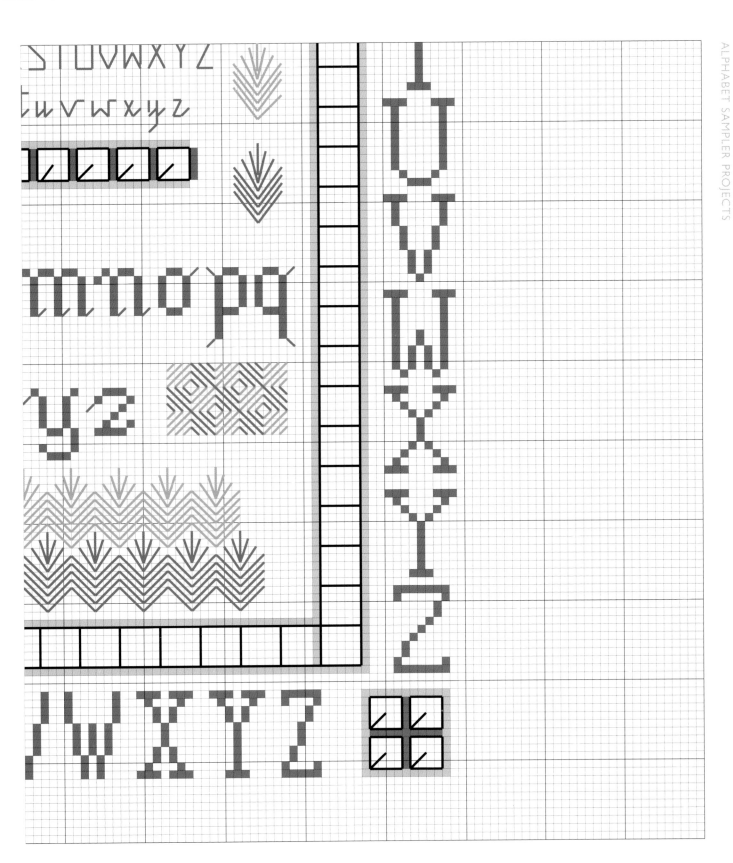

ALPHABET SAMPLER CARD

T his uses the same stitches, threads and fabric as the sampler, so it could be used as a practice piece.

Card details:

Cream, rectangular aperture 13.9 x 9.5cm (5½ x 3⅞in)

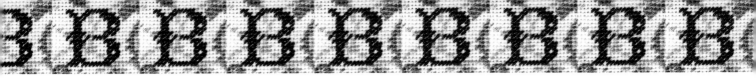

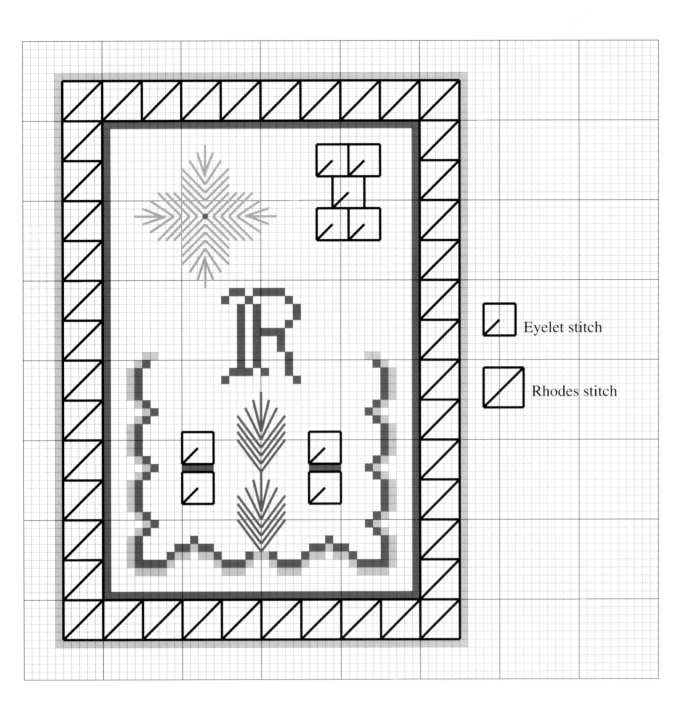

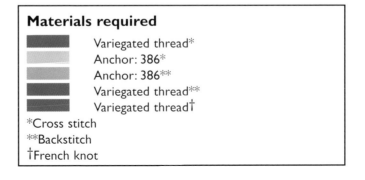

| | Eyelet stitch |
| | Rhodes stitch |

Design size	12.5 x 13.1cm (4⁹⁄₁₀ x 5³⁄₁₀in)
Fabric	28-count Jobelan
Fabric count	14 holes per inch
Stitch count	69 x 72
Stitch size	worked over 2 threads
Number of strands	2

Materials required

	Variegated thread*
	Anchor: 386*
	Anchor: 386**
	Variegated thread**
	Variegated thread†

*Cross stitch
**Backstitch
†French knot

149

MEDIEVAL ALPHABET SAMPLER AND CARDS

This sampler contrasts with the previous one. It is very bright and colourful, although a limited range of colours is used. The design is made up of individually decorated letters and riband labels adapted from a sixteenth century alphabet in a copy of the *Romant de la Rose*. Again, this is stitched on 28-count Jobelan over two threads, so 14-count fabric could be substituted. You will need a piece of fabric approximately 56 x 36in (22 x 14in).

I have used variegated thread from De Haviland in purple and pink, but these could be replaced by Anchor Stranded Cotton, numbers 100 and 65. To stitch the sampler you will need two skeins of 265, 152 and 268, and one skein of each of the other colours. Two strands of thread are used unless otherwise stated.

Start stitching in the centre so that the completed stitching will be in the centre of the fabric. When complete, press well on the wrong side on a padded surface using a damp cloth, then stretch and frame to your requirements.

This sampler gives the opportunity to stitch each decorated letter individually or stitch a message or, alternatively, a complete sampler. I have stitched three letters on different count fabric to demonstrate the contrast in size of the completed cards.

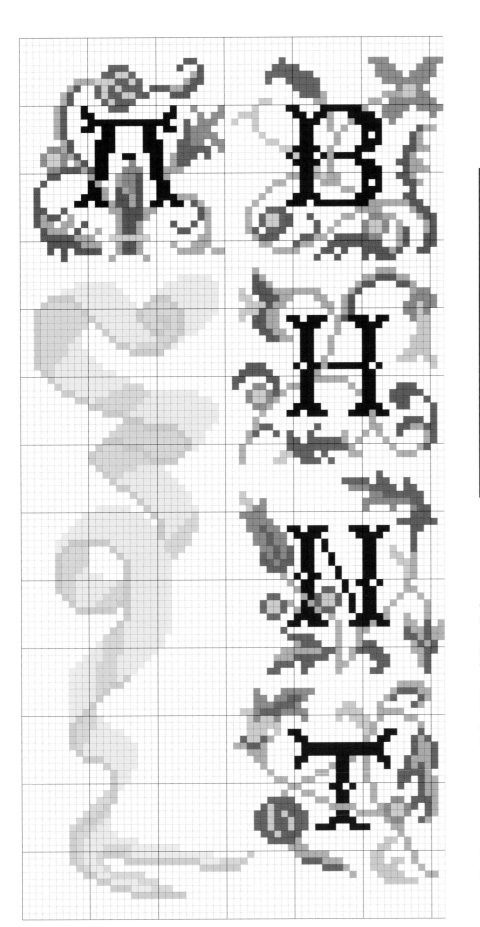

Materials required

▮	Anchor: 152
▮	Anchor: 265
▮	Anchor: 268
▮	De Haviland: purple
▮	De Haviland: pink
▮	Anchor Lamé: 303*
▮	Anchor: 297**, Lamé†
▮	Anchor: 298**, Lamé†

*Use 4 strands
**Use 2 strands
†Use 1 strand

Design size	44.8 x 22.9cm (17⅝ x 9in)
Fabric	28-count Jobelan
Fabric count	14 holes per inch
Stitch	cross stitch
Stitch count	247 x 126
Stitch size	worked over 2 threads
Number of strands	2

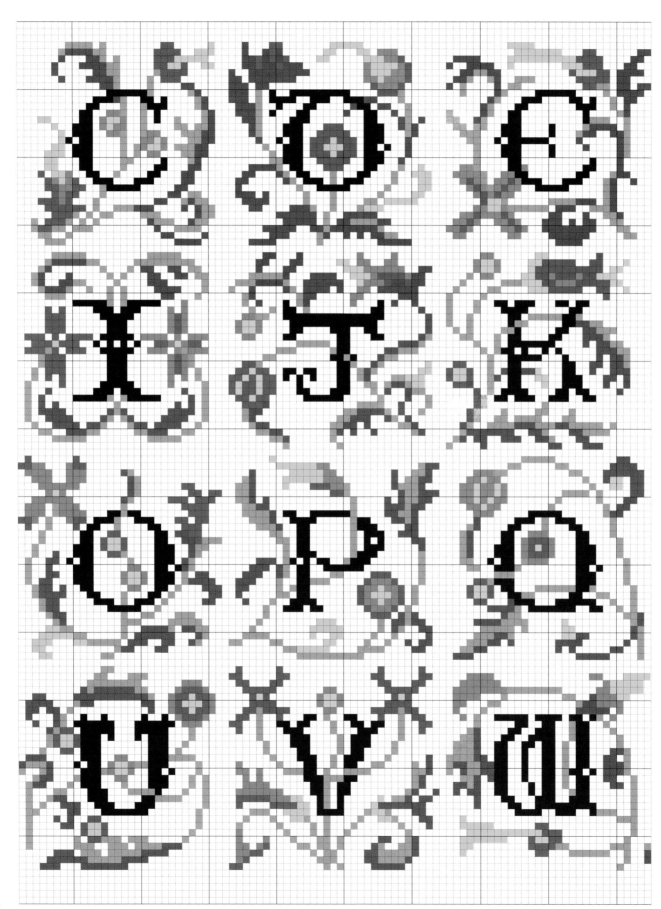

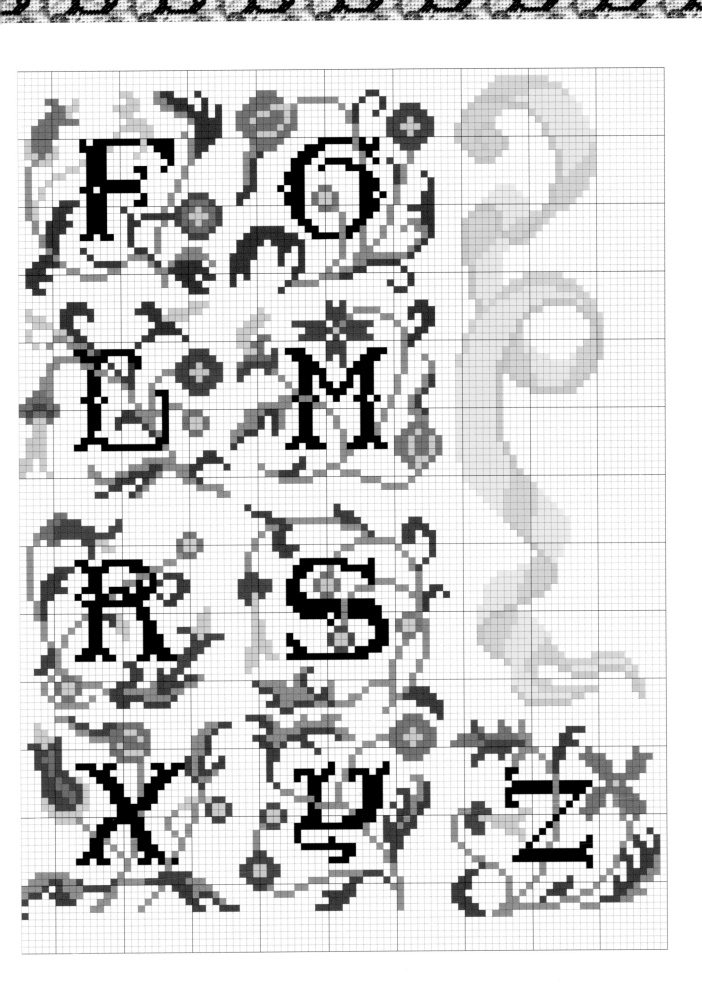

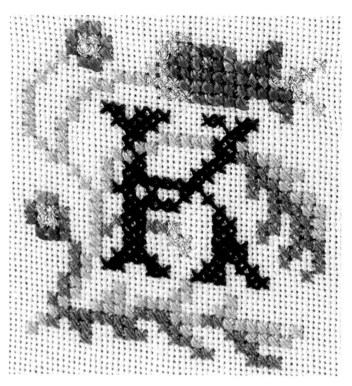
Card details:

Letter K   (14-count) dark green, square aperture 6.7cm (2⅝in)

Letter J   (16-count) gold, circular aperture 7cm (2⅜in)

Letter B   (22-count) bright white, square aperture 4cm (1½in)

VICTORIAN ALPHABET SAMPLER AND GIFT TAGS

This design is based on snippets of old Victorian samplers and put together with different alphabets to give a lovely country-style sampler.

The sampler is worked in Anchor Stranded Cotton, and to complete the stitching you will need two skeins of 236, 878 and 895, and one of each of the other colours. Two strands of thread are used throughout.

The fabric used is 28-count Jobelan, worked over two threads to give a 14-count. You will need a piece of fabric approximately 51 x 51cm (20 x 20in).

Start the stitching in the centre and work outwards until it is complete, then press on the wrong side on a padded surface using a damp cloth. Stretch and frame as required.

I have taken small motifs from the sampler to make gift tags, and they look wonderful in these textured tags from Framecraft.

Card details:

Cream gift tags, circular aperture 3.2cm (1¼in)

Design size	37.6 x 37cm (14⅞ x 14½in)
Fabric	28-count Jobelan
Fabric count	14 holes per inch
Stitch	cross stitch
Stitch count	207 x 204
Stitch size	worked over 2 threads
Number of strands	2

Materials required	
	Anchor: 236
	Anchor: 376
	Anchor: 378
	Anchor: 386
	Anchor: 875
	Anchor: 878
	Anchor: 894
	Anchor: 895
	Anchor: 896
	Anchor: 379

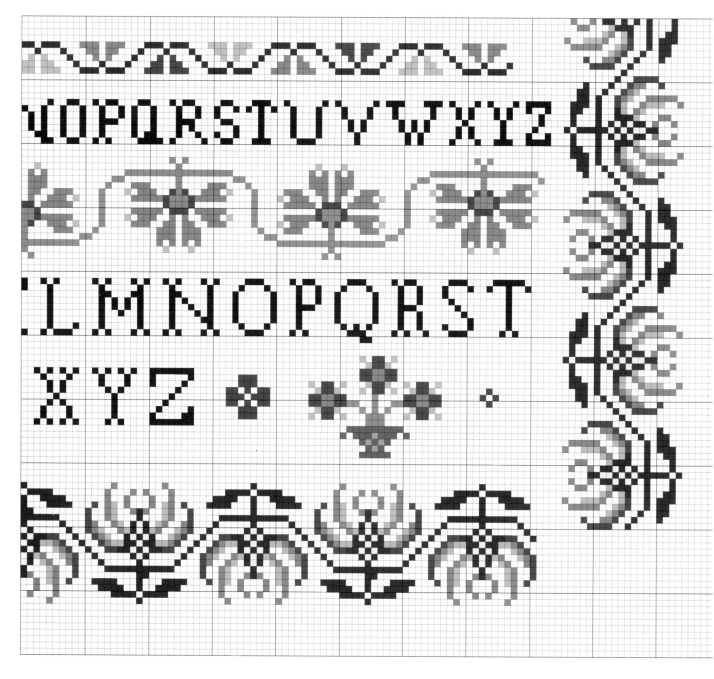

GRAPH PAPER

This graph paper can be photocopied and used to chart any messages
you wish to add to the card designs.

THREAD CONVERSION CHART

This conversion chart is for guidance only, as exact comparisons are not always possible.

Anchor	DMC	Madeira	Anchor	DMC	Madeira	Anchor	DMC	Madeira	Anchor	DMC	Madeira
1	blanc	2401	162	825	1107	330	947	205	894	3326	813
6	353	2605	164	824	2505	332	946	207	895	223	812
8	3824	304	185	964	1112	333	608	206	896	315	810
10	351	406	186	959	1113	334	606	209	897	221	2606
13	347	211	188	943	2706	335	606	209	899	3022	1906
19	817	407	189	991	2705	337	922	403	903	3032	2002
20	3777	2502	205	912	1213	341	355	314	905	3021	1904
22	815	2501	206	564	1210	343	932	1710	968	778	808
35	3705	411	214	368	2604	349	301	2306	969	816	809
38	3731	611	215	320	1310	351	400	2304	970	3726	2609
45	814	2606	216	367	1310	352	300	2304	1012	948	305
46	6566	210	217	319	1312	357	975	2602	1014	355	2502
47	304	510	227	701	1305	358	801	2008	1021	963	404
49	3689	607	236	3799	1713	359	898	2007	1023	760	405
50	605	613	241	703	1307	360	938	2005	1024	3328	406
52	957	2707	245	701	1305	368	436	2011	1025	347	407
54	956	611	246	986	1404	369	435	2010	1027	223	812
68	3687	604	253	772	1604	371	433	2602	1036	336	1712
69	3685	2609	254	3348	1409	372	738	2013	1037	3756	2504
70	*	2608	255	907	1410	376	842	1910	1042	369	1701
74	3354	606	256	906	1411	378	841	2601	1070	993	
75	3733	505	264	3348	1409	379	840	2601	1072	993	
76	961	505	265	471	1308	380	838	2005	1074	3814	
78	600	2609	266	470	1502	382	3371	2004	1089	996	
85	3609	710	267	469	1503	386	746	2512	1090	996	
94	917	706	268	937	1504	390	822	1908	5975	356	401
97	554	711	269	895	1507	397	3204	1901	1335		
99	552	2714	276	3770	2314	398	415	1802	1345		
101	550	713	278	472	1414	400	317	1714			
102	*	2709	279	734	1610	403	310	2400			
108	210	2711	280	581	1611	683	890	1705			
109	209	2711	289	307	103	781					
112	*	2710	292	3078	102	842	3013	1605			
117	341	901	293	727	110	843	3012	1606			
118	340	902	295	726	109	846	936	1507			
122	3807	2702	297	973	105	847	928	1805			
127	823	1008	298	972	107	850	926	1707			
137	798	911	300	677	111	856	370	1509			
139	797	912	303	742	114	858	524	1512			
140	3755	910	305	743	109	871	3041	806			
145	799	910	306	725	2514	876	503	1703			
146	798	911	307	783	2514	877	502	1205			
147	797	912	309	781	2213	878	501	1205			
149	336	1006	311	977	2301	879	500	1204			
150	823	1007	314	741	203	885	739	2014			
152	939	1009	316	740	202	887	3046	2206			
160	813	1105	323	722	307	888	3045	2112			
161	826	1012	326	720	309	889	610	2105			

INDEX

ABOUT THE AUTHOR

Carol was born in Scarborough, North Yorkshire. For many years she lived in the East Riding of Yorkshire with her husband Alan and two daughters, but has recently moved to Staffordshire.

She has always been interested in embroidery and design and with a friend started a needlework kit business. This has now been sold, and for the last ten years Carol has been a freelance needlework designer, working mainly for magazines and kit companies.

She spends a lot of time walking in the Derbyshire Dales, but some form of embroidery is always at hand. Carol thinks that one of the nicest things about stitching is that it is so portable and can be done almost anywhere.

Carol has written three other books for the Guild of Master Craftsman: Celtic Cross-Stitch Designs, Making Miniature Chinese Rugs and Carpets and Cross-Stitch Designs from China. She is currently working on a fifth book, Cross-Stitch Designs from India, for publication in 2004.

TITLES AVAILABLE FROM

GMC Publications

BOOKS

WOODCARVING

Beginning Woodcarving   *GMC Publications*
Carving Architectural Detail in Wood: The Classical Tradition
    Frederick Wilbur
Carving Birds & Beasts   *GMC Publications*
Carving Classical Styles in Wood   *Frederick Wilbur*
Carving the Human Figure: Studies in Wood and Stone   *Dick Onians*
Carving Nature: Wildlife Studies in Wood   *Frank Fox-Wilson*
Celtic Carved Lovespoons: 30 Patterns   *Sharon Littley & Clive Griffin*
Decorative Woodcarving (New Edition)   *Jeremy Williams*
Elements of Woodcarving   *Chris Pye*
Figure Carving in Wood: Human and Animal Forms   *Sara Wilkinson*
Lettercarving in Wood: A Practical Course   *Chris Pye*
Relief Carving in Wood: A Practical Introduction   *Chris Pye*
Woodcarving for Beginners   *GMC Publications*
Woodcarving Made Easy   *Cynthia Rogers*
Woodcarving Tools, Materials & Equipment (New Edition in 2 vols.)
    Chris Pye

WOODTURNING

Bowl Turning Techniques Masterclass   *Tony Boase*
Chris Child's Projects for Woodturners   *Chris Child*
Decorating Turned Wood: The Maker's Eye   *Liz & Michael O'Donnell*
Green Woodwork   *Mike Abbott*
A Guide to Work-Holding on the Lathe   *Fred Holder*
Keith Rowley's Woodturning Projects   *Keith Rowley*
Making Screw Threads in Wood   *Fred Holder*
Segmented Turning: A Complete Guide   *Ron Hampton*
Turned Boxes: 50 Designs   *Chris Stott*
Turning Green Wood   *Michael O'Donnell*
Turning Pens and Pencils   *Kip Christensen & Rex Burningham*
Wood for Woodturners   *Mark Baker*
Woodturning: Forms and Materials   *John Hunnex*
Woodturning: A Foundation Course (New Edition)   *Keith Rowley*
Woodturning: A Fresh Approach   *Robert Chapman*
Woodturning: An Individual Approach   *Dave Regester*
Woodturning: A Source Book of Shapes   *John Hunnex*
Woodturning Masterclass   *Tony Boase*
Woodturning Projects: A Workshop Guide to Shapes   *Mark Baker*

WOODWORKING

Beginning Picture Marquetry   *Lawrence Threadgold*
Carcass Furniture   *GMC Publications*
Celtic Carved Lovespoons: 30 Patterns   *Sharon Littley & Clive Griffin*
Celtic Woodcraft   *Glenda Bennett*
Celtic Woodworking Projects   *Glenda Bennett*
Complete Woodfinishing (Revised Edition)   *Ian Hosker*
David Charlesworth's Furniture-Making Techniques
    David Charlesworth
David Charlesworth's Furniture-Making Techniques – Volume 2
    David Charlesworth
Furniture Projects with the Router   *Kevin Ley*
Furniture Restoration (Practical Crafts)   *Kevin Jan Bonner*

Furniture Restoration: A Professional at Work   *John Lloyd*
Furniture Workshop   *Kevin Ley*
Green Woodwork   *Mike Abbott*
History of Furniture: Ancient to 1900   *Michael Huntley*
Intarsia: 30 Patterns for the Scrollsaw   *John Everett*
Making Heirloom Boxes   *Peter Lloyd*
Making Screw Threads in Wood   *Fred Holder*
Making Woodwork Aids and Devices   *Robert Wearing*
Mastering the Router   *Ron Fox*
Pine Furniture Projects for the Home   *Dave Mackenzie*
Router Magic: Jigs, Fixtures and Tricks to
    Unleash your Router's Full Potential   *Bill Hylton*
Router Projects for the Home   *GMC Publications*
Router Tips & Techniques   *Robert Wearing*
Routing: A Workshop Handbook   *Anthony Bailey*
Routing for Beginners (Revised and Expanded Edition)   *Anthony Bailey*
Stickmaking: A Complete Course   *Andrew Jones & Clive George*
Stickmaking Handbook   *Andrew Jones & Clive George*
Storage Projects for the Router   *GMC Publications*
Veneering: A Complete Course   *Ian Hosker*
Veneering Handbook   *Ian Hosker*
Wood: Identification & Use   *Terry Porter*
Woodworking Techniques and Projects   *Anthony Bailey*
Woodworking with the Router: Professional
    Router Techniques any Woodworker can Use
    Bill Hylton & Fred Matlack

UPHOLSTERY

Upholstery: A Beginners' Guide   *David James*
Upholstery: A Complete Course (Revised Edition)   *David James*
Upholstery Restoration   *David James*
Upholstery Techniques & Projects   *David James*
Upholstery Tips and Hints   *David James*

DOLLS' HOUSES AND MINIATURES

1/12 Scale Character Figures for the Dolls' House   *James Carrington*
Americana in 1/12 Scale: 50 Authentic Projects
    Joanne Ogreenc & Mary Lou Santovec
The Authentic Georgian Dolls' House   *Brian Long*
A Beginners' Guide to the Dolls' House Hobby   *Jean Nisbett*
Celtic, Medieval and Tudor Wall Hangings in 1/12 Scale Needlepoint
    Sandra Whitehead
Creating Decorative Fabrics: Projects in 1/12 Scale   *Janet Storey*
Dolls' House Accessories, Fixtures and Fittings   *Andrea Barham*
Dolls' House Furniture: Easy-to-Make Projects in 1/12 Scale   *Freida Gray*
Dolls' House Makeovers   *Jean Nisbett*
Dolls' House Window Treatments   *Eve Harwood*
Edwardian-Style Hand-Knitted Fashion for 1/12 Scale Dolls
    Yvonne Wakefield
How to Make Your Dolls' House Special: Fresh Ideas for Decorating
    Beryl Armstrong
Making 1/12 Scale Wicker Furniture for the Dolls' House   *Sheila Smith*
Making Miniature Chinese Rugs and Carpets   *Carol Phillipson*
Making Miniature Food and Market Stalls   *Angie Scarr*

CRAFTS

GARDENING

PHOTOGRAPHY

ART TECHNIQUES

VIDEOS

MAGAZINES

WOODTURNING ✦ WOODCARVING ✦ FURNITURE & CABINETMAKING
THE ROUTER ✦ NEW WOODWORKING ✦ THE DOLLS' HOUSE MAGAZINE
OUTDOOR PHOTOGRAPHY ✦ BLACK & WHITE PHOTOGRAPHY
MACHINE KNITTING NEWS ✦ KNITTING
GUILD OF MASTER CRAFTSMEN NEWS

The above represents a full list of all titles currently published or scheduled to be published.
All are available direct from the Publishers or through bookshops, newsagents and specialist retailers.
To place an order, or to obtain a complete catalogue, contact:

GMC Publications,
Castle Place, 166 High Street, Lewes, East Sussex BN7 1XU United Kingdom
Tel: 01273 488005 Fax: 01273 402866
E-mail: pubs@thegmcgroup.com Website: www.gmcbooks.com

Orders by credit card are accepted